practical CLASSICS
& CAR RESTORER

E-Type Jaguar Restoration

Published by

KELSEY PUBLISHING LIMITED

Printed in Great Britain by
Spin Offset Limited, New Road,
Rainham, Essex for
Kelsey Publishing Limited, Kelsey House,
77 High Street, Beckenham, Kent BR3 1AN.
on behalf of PPG Publishing Limited.

© 1991

ISBN 1873098 03 0

Acknowledgements

Over the course of our 'E' type restoration a number of people have offered assistance. In particular we would like to thank; Gallaher Tobacco Ltd. for their sponsorship, Vintage Tyre Supplies Ltd. of Middlesex for the tyres, Martin Robey Sales Ltd. of Warwickshire for panels and parts, Glasurit Paints of Middlesex for the paint, Bells Silencer Services Ltd. of Wiltshire for the exhaust, Rovercraft of Kent for machining the engine, Barry Hankinson of Hereford for the trim, London Chroming of London for rechroming, Metalock of Kent for the engine block repair, Burlen Fuel Systems of Wiltshire for carburettor parts, Lynx Cars of Hastings for the roof panel, Abacus Autoglaziers of Orpington for fitting the windscreens, NLS Spares of Barking and RM & J Smith of Crewe for various 'bits and bobs', The Jaguar Enthusiasts Club for use of their special tools and finally Colin Ford who we must congratulate on the completion of the car and thank for his hard work and persistence throughout the project.

Buying guide written and photographed by Paul Skilleter.
Restoration written and photographed by Phil Cooper.
Bonnet repair written and photographed by John Williams.

Introduction

The E-Type Jaguar project was one of the most thrilling restorations ever undertaken by *Practical Classics & Car Restorer* magazine and this is reflected in every page of the unique coverage in this book.

The strength of the book is greatly added to by Paul Skilleter's exhaustive work of research on the E-Type production changes, which will aid many restorers in "getting it right". Also Paul's supplement which makes an invaluable and entertaining general reference and an ideal introduction into the restoration itself.

For the purposes of the actual restoration project the bonnet was not restored (it was missing from the project car and a new one had to be purchased). We therefore added an earlier two-part article by John Williams, which must stand as the best explanation to this daunting task that has ever been written.

The opportunity to use colour throughout the whole coverage of the project enhanced the series tremendously and Phil Cooper's photography, particularly his "heading" shots, injects great excitement into the whole book.

We believe that not only those seriously contemplating undertaking an E-Type restoration project, but also anyone who may wonder what such a project would entail, will find this book fascinating and absorbing.

GW

Contents

All prices in this book were current only at the time that the reprinted articles originally appeared (c1990).

EVOLUTION
E-TYPE PRODUCTION CHANGES

Abbreviations: FHC – Fixed Head Coupe   OTS – Open Two Seater   2P2 – Two-Plus-Two   Rhd – Right-Hand-Drive   Lhd – Left-Hand-Drive

3.8 E-type

CHASSIS	Date	Chassis No. Rhd	Chassis No. Lhd
Water deflector fitted on front stub-axle carrier	Aug 1961 (FHC) (OTS)	860001 850048	885001 875133
Self-adjusting handbrake introduced	Oct 1961	860004 850090 875332	885015
Larger rear outer hub-bearings	Oct 1961	850005 850092	885021 875386
Larger universal-joint on prop-shaft	Oct 1961	860006 850104	885026 875496
Longer rear road springs	Oct 1961	860008 850137	885039 875542
Brass bush in brake and clutch pedal housing	Dec 1961	860021	885105
Brass bush in brake and clutch pedal housing replaced by impregnated plastic – lubrication no longer required	Dec 1961	860021 850233	885105 875859
Modified brake master-cylinders to incorporate positive location of spring support to piston	Jan 1962	860027 850255	885156 876015
Change of brake-pad material of Mintex M33	Jan 1962	–	–
Brake power lever and pedals altered to increase mechanical advantage Accelerator pedal on Rhd cars altered to facilitate 'heel and toe' operation	May 1962	860387 850475	885871 876999
'Sealed for life' universal-joints on prop-shaft	May 1962	860387 850480	885888 877045
New oil-seal container and felt oil-seal fitted to outer fulcrum shaft	June 1962	860451 850504	885985 877183
Modified clutch master-cylinder to incorporate positive location of rear spring support to piston	July 1962	860647 858548	886219 877489
Once-piece forged lower steering column to replace tubular-shaft assembly	July 1962	860647 850548	886214 877488
Solid forged rear-axle half-shafts to replace tubular shafts	July 1962	860658 850555	886247 877550
Handbrake cable, compensator and calipers modified	July 1962	860664	886263
Revised fixing for rear-brake calipers	Sept 1962	860741 850578	886456 877736
Change of rear axle-ratio – USA and Canada now 3.31:1, home market and other countries now 3.07:1. Option of 2.93:1 deleted	Oct 1962	–	–
'Sealed for life' rear-axle half-shaft joints	Dec 1962	–	–
Water thrower fitted to rear hubs	Sept 1962	860833 850584	886686 877964
Thicker (½inch) rear brake discs with new calipers and modified caliper mountings and final-drive casing. Incorporated by axle ratio	June 1963 3.54:1 3.31:1 3.07:1	861185 850722	888673 879441 888695 879461 888706 879461
Handbrake compensator inner lever ink replaced by inner fork-end and outer fork-end giving greater range of adjustment	Aug 1963	861203 850728	888760 879551
Change of rear-axle ratio: USA and Canada 3.54:1	Sept 1963 (plus (plus	888952 to 888994) 879751 to 879808)	889124 880026
Italy, France, Belgium, Germany and Holland 3.07:1			888967 879759
Home market and countries not included above 3.31:1		861226 850737	889003 879821
New rear-axle breather unit – valve replaced by extension assembly	Nov 1963	861364 850785	889452 880562
Half-shaft universal-joint shrouds	Jan 1964	861424 850806	889698 880755
Brake-fluid reservoir cap fitted with cover	Jan 1964	861427 850657	889697 880760

ENGINE AND GEARBOX

	Date	Engine or Chassis No. Rhd	Engine or Chassis No. Lhd
Larger oil pump	June 1961	R.1009	
Cast-iron crankshaft pulley instead of alloy	Oct 1961	R.1459	
Automatic fan-belt tensioner	Oct 1961	R.11845	
C42 dynamo and RB340 regulator fitted. New petrol-pump assembly and tank with modified tank filter and one-piece drain plug	Oct 1961	860005 850092	885021 875387
New crankshaft rear oil seal (asbestos rope)	Dec 1961	R.2564	
Revised throttle arrangement with two slave-shafts instead of three, and flexible coupling etc. deleted. Air balance-pipe redesigned with two bosses instead of three	Jan 1962	R.2934	
Reduced big-end clearances	Feb 1962	R.3162	
Modified cylinder-head gasket with enlarged head stud holes	Mar 1962	R.3691	
Drilled inlet camshaft to reduce cold-starting noise	May 1962	R.5001	
Duplex water-pump belt with modified pulleys	June 1962	R.5250	
Modified sump-filter basket incorporating four semi-circular cutouts	June 1962	R.5400	
Revised clutch-fluid reservoir and brackets	July 1962	860678 850556	886283 877557
Internal fuel-pipe material changed from Vulkollan to Nylon	Sept 1962	860584 850527	886095 877355
Longer inlet-valve guides	Sept 1962	R.6724	
Modified piston rings and connecting-rod with additional big-end lug drillings	Sept 1962	R.7104	
Larger main-bearing cap dowels	Oct 1962	R.7195	
Quick-left thermostat	Nov 1962	R.8300	

Modified mounting at rear of gearbox	Jan 1963	861062 850647	888082 878889
Radiator header-tank revised with higher-pressure (9lbs) radiator cap	March 1963	861091 850657	888241 879044
Straight instead of convoluted header tank hose		–	
Delrin needle-valve fitted to carburettors with new float-chamber lid and hinged lever	June 1963	RA.2464	
New-type (22 D6 instead DMBZ6) distributor	June 1963	–	
Modified oil pump and ¾-inch instead 1¹⁄₁₆inch oil suction pipe	June 1963	RA.2078	
Exhaust valves of improved material	Sept 1963	RA.2972	
Modified piston with chamfer and oil drain holes below control ring to improve oil consumption	Mar 1964	RA.5649	
Laycock diaphragm clutch introduced (modified flywheel to suit both Borg & Beck and Laycocks clutches)	Mar 1964	RA.5801	
Intermediate lower timing chain damper secured to bosses in block instead of to timing-chain bracket	May 1964	RA.6025	
Modified distributor (Lucas No. 40888A) fitted to 9:1 engines	June 1964	RA.6834	

BODY AND FITTINGS

		Chassis No.	
		Rhd	Lhd
Internal bonnet locks	Sept 1961 FHC OTS	860005 850092	885021 875386
Seat-belt attachments points provided	Jan 1962	860113 850301	885318 875359
Revised method of attaching bonnet-hinges to front subframe with bolt retaining hinges to cross-tube	Feb 1962	860139 850239	885385 876458
Heel wells fitted. Body Nos: 1635 1647 2879 2889	Feb 1962	860176 850358	885504 876582
Combined ignition switch and steering lock fitted to all cars exported to Germany.	Mar 1962		885567 876665
Electrically heated backlight optional	April 1962	–	–

		Chassis No.	
Detachable hardtop available	May 1962	–	–
Minor body changes, FHC only, to outer rear wings, bootlid gutter, bootlid shell, hinge for bootlid, tail panel, lid for petrol filler, door shell, door light, etc.	May 1962	860476	886014
Alteration to OTS door (requiring revised chrome outer finisher)	May 1962	850507	877202
New rear bulkhead-section to allow extra rearward travel for seats; temporary modification had been incorporated in driver's side only shortly after car's introduction	June 1962	860581 850527	886093 877356
Revised jack of cantilever type	June 1962	860661 850549	886247 877519
Pattern change on embossed aluminium finishers on instrument panel, front finisher panel, gearbox cover	Oct 1962	860913 850610	887132 878302
Revised bootlid prop on FHC	Dec 1962	861014	887317
Improved quarter-light catches to prevent closing at speed on FHC	Oct 1963	–	–
Modification to allow opening of OTS boot if cable fails (via hole in numberplate panel using ³⁄₁₆inch diameter right-angle rod)	Jan 1964	850768	880291

NOTES – 3.8 E-Type

i   When the optional close-ratio gearbox is fitted, a different clutch-housing, primary shaft and oil-seal are used.

ii   Dunlop SP radial tyres were offered as optional equipment from May 1963.

iii   Manufacture of the Lucas immersed centrifugal impeller fuel pump ceased during the early-seventies, and the factory issued a kit to convert the fuel system to the external SU reciprocating-diaphragm pump (type LAUF 301) similar to that used on 4.2 cars. Position for the SU pump was in the right-hand corner of the spare-wheel well, adjacent to the rear-wheel arch.

iv   Wing mirrors (Part No. C.19909) were available as optional extras from 1961 (front-wing mounting).

v   In 1962 a booklet was issued by the works entitled Tuning and Preparation of E-type Cars for Competition use (now out of print). It listed various minor body and mechanical alterations and a number of special parts available from the factory.

4.2 Series 1 E-type

CHASSIS

	Date Rhd	Chassis No. Lhd	
Front disc-brake shields fitted	Feb 1965 FHC	1E.20100	1E.30302
Change of axle ratio from 3.31:1 to 3.07:1 (except USA and Canada, (3.54:1)	April 1965 FHC OTS	1E.20329 1E.1152	1E.30772 1E.1073
7-tooth pinion introduced to improve steering when radial-ply tyres fitted	Mar 1966	1E.220993 1E.1413	1E.31765 1E.11535
New road wheel introduced with forged centre hub and straight spokes	May 1967 2P2	1E.21518 1E.1814 1E.50912	1E.34339 1E.11535 1E.77475
Powr-Lok diff. discontinued as standard except USA 3.54	Sept 1967	1E.21620 1E.1887	1E.34603 1E.15982
Grease nipples reintroduced on half-shaft universal joints	Jan 1968	1E.21669 1E.1926 1E.51067	1E.34851 1E.16721 1E.77705

ENGINE AND GEARBOX

		Engine or Chassis No.	
		Rhd	Lhd
Chamfered idler gear to reduce possible gearbox noise	Nov 1964	–	–
Modified roller-bearing fitted to gearbox constant-pinion shaft	Mar 1965	EJ.945	
Constant-pinion shaft changed to include oil thrower	Feb. 1966	EJ.3170	
New brake and clutch master-cylinders and pedal housings fitted to standardise with 2-plus-2	Mar 1966	1E.21000 1E.1413	1E.32010 1E.11741
Shield fitted to alternator	May 1966	7E.6333	
Modified carburettor assembly with low-lift cam to reduce engine speed when choke operated	Sept 1966 2P2	7E.7298 7E.50022	
Retaining washer fitted to additionally secure gear-lever	Nov 1966	EJ.7920	

6

	Date	Chassis No. Rhd	Lhd
Modified clutch and brake master-cylinders with shorter	Nov 1966	1E.21342 1E.1561	1E.32942 1E.13011
Pushrods to revise pedal angles also improve accelerator-pedal angle		?	?
Valve-guides fitted with circlips to ensure positive location in cylinder-head	Jan 1967	7E.7450 7E.50022	
Oil seals fitted to inlet-valve guides	Mar 1967	7E.11668 7E.52687	
US Federal spec. introduced	Jan 1968		1E.34583 1E.15180
Replaceable filter fitted to fuel line	Feb. 1968	1E.21662 1E.1905 1E.50143	1E.34772 1E.16057 1E.77701
Vertical-flow radiator, new water-pump assembly, twin cooling-fans with relay, revised breather-pipe and thermostat (already incorporated in LHD cars)	April 1968	1E.31807 1E.2051 1E.51213	
Solid-skirt Hepworth and Grandage pistons fitted instead of Brico split-skirt	June 1968	– –	– –
Revised water-pump pulley and belt to increase pump speed and flow-rate	June 1968	7E.17158 7E.54837	

BODY AND FITTINGS

	Date	Chassis No. Rhd	Lhd
Revision of finisher-panel assembly on gearbox and prop-shaft tunnel, deletion of chrome bezel at top of panel for gearlever gauntlet and chrome ferrel at top of gauntlet	Nov 1964	1E.10360 1E.1061	
Pocket under rear side	Jan 1965	1E.20117	1E.30402

	Date	Rhd	Lhd
windows deleted. Change from mocquette to plastic on rear wheelarches, rear door hinges, etc (FHC)			
Hazard warning light fitted as standard	Dec 1965	1E.12025	1E.32194
Window-frame seals changed from felt to flocked runner (FHC)	Feb 1966	1E.20953	1E.31920
Switch incorporated in heated back-light circuit	April 1966	1E.21223	1E.32609
Ambla gear-lever gauntlet		1E.21442 1E.1686 1E.50586	1E.33549 1E.13589 1E.76911
Deletion of headlight covers	July 1967	1E.21584 1E.1864 1E.50975	1E.34250 1E.15889 1E.77645
Revised dash assembly incl. heater box and controls, cubby box lid, choke, switches	April	1E.21784 1E.2039	
US Federal spec. doors, casings and linings fitted to RHD cars	June 1968	–	–
Water-temperature gauge with zonal markings only replacing calibrated gauge	July 1968	–	1E.34945 1E.16538 1E.77838

NOTES – 4.2 SERIES 1 E-TYPE

i   Oil-cooler and installation kit for 3.8 and 4.2 cars (not Series 2) available as an extra from April 1969.

ii From late-1967/early-1968 various updating features were incorporated into the 4.2 E-type's specification; although colloquially known as the 'Series 1½', these changes did not denote a new model as such, and it is not possible to define a distinct '1½' specification because of progressive modifications carried out before the appearance of the true Series 2 car.

iii Close-ratio gearbox discontinued commencing box no. EE 1001.

iv Cars with air-conditioning have sealant cooling system, with expansion tank having 13lb cap mounted on bulkhead (header tank still retained) June 1967.

4.2 Series 2 E-type

CHASSIS	Date	Chassis No. Rhd	Lhd
Non-eared hub-caps standardized on RHD cars	Jan 1969 FHC OTS 2P2	1R.200073 1R.1054 1R.1054 1R.35099	
Revised handbrake-lever assembly introduced with increased length and end portion angled upwards (2-Plus-2)	May 1970	1R.35816	1R.43924
Larger-diameter torsion-bars fitted to RHD cars (0.744-inch to 0.780-inch)	Aug 1970	1R.1776 1R.20955	

ENGINE AND GEARBOX

	Date	Engine or Chassis No. Rhd	Lhd
Lucas 11AC alternator with side-entry cables	Jan 1969	1R.20007 1R.1013 1R.35011	1R.25284 1R.7443 1R.40208
Improved clutch with higher-rated diaphragm spring to reduce tendency to slip	Mar 1969 2P2	7R.2588 7R.35731	
'Load-shedding' ignition/starter switch introduced (isolates most auxiliaries while starter engaged)	April 1969	1R.26533 1R.9860 1R.42382	
Camshaft covers secured by countersunk screw at front centre position	May 1969	7R.4159 7R.36600	
Cylinder-block drain tap replaced by plug	June 1969	7R.5542 7R.37655	
Engine No. stamping relocated on crankcase bellhousing flange on LH side of engine, adjacent dip-stick	Aug 1969	7R.6306 7R.38106	

	Date	Rhd	Lhd
New camshafts with redesigned profiles to give quieter valve operation over wider range of valve clearances and longer periods between adjustment	Nov 1969	7R.8688 7R.388855	
Camshaft covers drilled for warm-air duct (fitted on emission engines)	Jan 1970	7R.8768 7R.38895	
Ballast-resistor ignition fitted	Jan 1970	1R.20486 1R.1393	1R.27051 1R.11052
Key alarm facility ignition switch, USA/Canada	Jan 1970	1R.35643	1R.42850
Revised clutch-operating rod to accommodate wider setting tolerances	Mar 1970	7R.9710 7R.39112	
New crankshaft distance-piece with 'O' ring	Aug 1970	7R.13199 7R.40326	
Revised thermostat (OTS and FHC)	Oct 1970	7R.140440	
Revised exhaust camshaft without oilway drilling in back of cams, to reduce oil consumption (OTS and FHC)	Oct 1970	7R.14075	

BODY AND FITTINGS

	Date	Chassis No. Rhd	Lhd
Steering-column lock fitted to RHD cars	Dec 1968 FHC OTS	1R.20095 1R.35099	
Gas-filled bonnet stay	June 1969	1R.20270 1R.1188 1R.35353	1R.26387 1R.9570 1R.42118
Petrol tank with design modification to upper panel	Mar 1969	1R.20119 1R.1068 1R.35798	1R.25524 1R.7993 1R.406688

		Rhd	Lhd
Perforated leather trim and modified head restraints	May 1969	1R.20212 1R.1138	1R.26005 1R.8869
Provision for head restraints in seats	Aug 1969	1R.20366 1R.1302 1R.35458	1R.26684 1R.10152 1R.42560
Mercury-cell clock replaced by battery-operated instrument	Oct 1969	1R.24425 1R.1351 1R.35564	1R.26835 1R.10537 1R.42677
Demister-tube extension fitted to 2-plus-2	Oct 1969	1R.35650	1R.42552
Key-alarm facility ignition switch (USA cars)	May 1970		

NOTES – 4.2 SERIES 2 E-TYPE

i   Close-ratio gearbox available as optional extra (Part No. C.28648).
ii New model year 70/71 identified on Federal cars by changing prefix on some cars to 2R.

5.3 Series 3 E-type

CHASSIS

		Chassis No.	
		Rhd	Lhd
Modified brake-pedal components to improve left-foot clearance (RHD automatic cars only)	July 1971 2P2 OTS	1S.50176 1S.1005	
Handbrake assembly made common to RHD and LHD cars	Dec 1971	1S.50872 1S.1152	1S.72357 1S.20122
3.07:1 axle offered as alternative to 3.31:1 on manual cars	April 1972	–	–
Revised adjuster-cam with larger cam profile on torsion-bar	June 1972	1S.51263 1S.1348	1S.73372 1S.20569
Modified pinion-valve assembly on rack and pinion due to isolated instances of self-steer	Dec 1972	1S.51318 1S.1443	1S.73721 1S.20921
Revised power rack and pinion assembly ('W' prefix)	Jan 1973		
Axle ratio on all USA/Canada cars now 3.31:1 (3.54:1 no longer fitted to manual cars); 3.07:1 fitted for all other countries	Mar 1973	– 1S.21576	1S.74261
Two-outlet exhaust-pipe with modified silencer replacing four-outlet 'fantail' pipe	Mar 1973	1S.51318 1S.1741	1S.74662 1S.22046
Phosphor-bronze rear hub-spacer replacing steel spacer to eliminate 'click' in rear suspension	June 1973	–	–

ENGINE AND GEARBOX

		Engine or Chassis No.	
		Rhd	Lhd
Modified crankshaft thrust-washer	Dec 1971	7S.4510	
Improved piston assembly (lighter)	May 1972	7S.6310	
Revised starter motor and flywheel (driven plate on automatic cars)	May 1972	7S.7001	
Forward section of engine rainshield now secured to an additional support mounted on front inlet manifold	June 1972	1S.51247 1S.1304	1S.73337 1S.20558
Revised shell bearings to connecting-rod big-ends – oil feed-hole deleted	June 1972	7S.7155	
Printed-circuit ballast resistor (Lucas No. 47229) introduced	Aug 1972	7S.7560	
N10Y plugs specified instead of N9Y	Oct 1972	–	–
Modified water-pump and simplified water-hose system	Oct 1972	7S.7785	
Deletion of small-end oil-feed drilling in connecting-rods	Oct 1972	7S.7856	
Revised main bearings with improved lining material	Dec 1972	7S.8189	
Sealed fuel-system with carbon cannister	Dec 1972	1S.21029	
New needle-roller bearings in gearbox	Jan 1973	KL.4241	
Thermostatic vacuum switch fitted to RH rear coolant branch-pipe and associated hoses deleted from all non-exhaust-emission engines	Feb 1973	7S.8444	
New air-injection pump with integral air filter fitted to all exhaust-emission engines	Feb 1973	7S.9034	
Coil-and-ballast resistor moved to RH rear of engine for improved accessability to engine drive-belts	Feb 1973	7S.9679	
Revised Borg-Warner Model 12 automatic gearbox fitted, identical to XJ12-type	Feb 1973	7S.9715	
New petrol-filter assembly with metal filter bowl, dispensing with fuel stop tap. Filter relocated to extreme right of luggage-boot bulkhead panel	Mar 1973	1S.51617 1S.1665	1S.74312 1S.21662
Engines to ECE 15 European emissions spec. for Germany only	Mar 1973		1S.74769 1S.22272
XJ12 crankshaft damper fitted for standardization	May 1973	7S.10799	
Improved oil-pump assembly with new housing	July 1973	7S.12065	
Cars for USA/Canada fitted with revised camshaft with different cam profile	Oct 1973	7S.1400	
Modified synchromesh-operating sleeve to prevent jumping out of forward gears	Oct 1973	7S.14000	KL.6772
New gearbox countershaft of revised material	Oct 1973	7S.14341	KL.7098
High-load coil and amplifier to improve plug performance	Feb 1974	7S.16210	
Engines to ECE 15 European emissions spec. to all markets except USA/Canada/Japan (OTS)	Oct 1974	1S.2450	1S.23419
Revised valve tappets	Nov 1974	7S.17074	

BODY AND FITTINGS

		Chassis No.	
		Rhd	Lhd
Red marking deleted from water-temperature gauge (USA cars)	July 1971	– –	1S.71370 1S.20025
Connector inserted in windscreen-washer tubing to facilitate removal of bonnet	Nov 1971 2P2 OTS	1S.50203 1S.1005	1S.71476 1S.20025
Demister flap controlled by short cable and connecting-rod instead cable and pinion gears	Mar 1972	1S.50875 1S.1163	1S.72450 1S.20135
Improved symmetrical heater and choke controls	Mar 1972	1S.50379 1S.1040	1S.72319 1S.10091
Securing brackets fitted to centre cross-beam and lower rear-damper mounting for shipping (not towing)	April 1972	1S.50968 1S.1210	1S.72662 1S.20169
Fresh-air vents fitted, with control levers in cockpit	April 1972	1S.51016 1S.1236	1S.72682 1S.20173
Waso steering-column lock fitted in place of Britax	April 1972	1S.51049 1S.1232	1S.72687 1S.20175
Remote-control door mirror fitted to all USA/Canada cars	April 1972	–	1S.72661 1S.20169
Seat-belt alarm system fitted to USA cars, rear seats fixed	May 1972	–	1S.72661 1S.20169
Revised air ducts to rear brakes with increased ground clearance; now fitted during assembly and no longer supplied for dealer to fit	April 1973	1S.51610 1S.1663	1S.74266 1S.21606
Five-mph impact front and rear overriders introduced, USA	1974	–	1S.74586 1S.23240

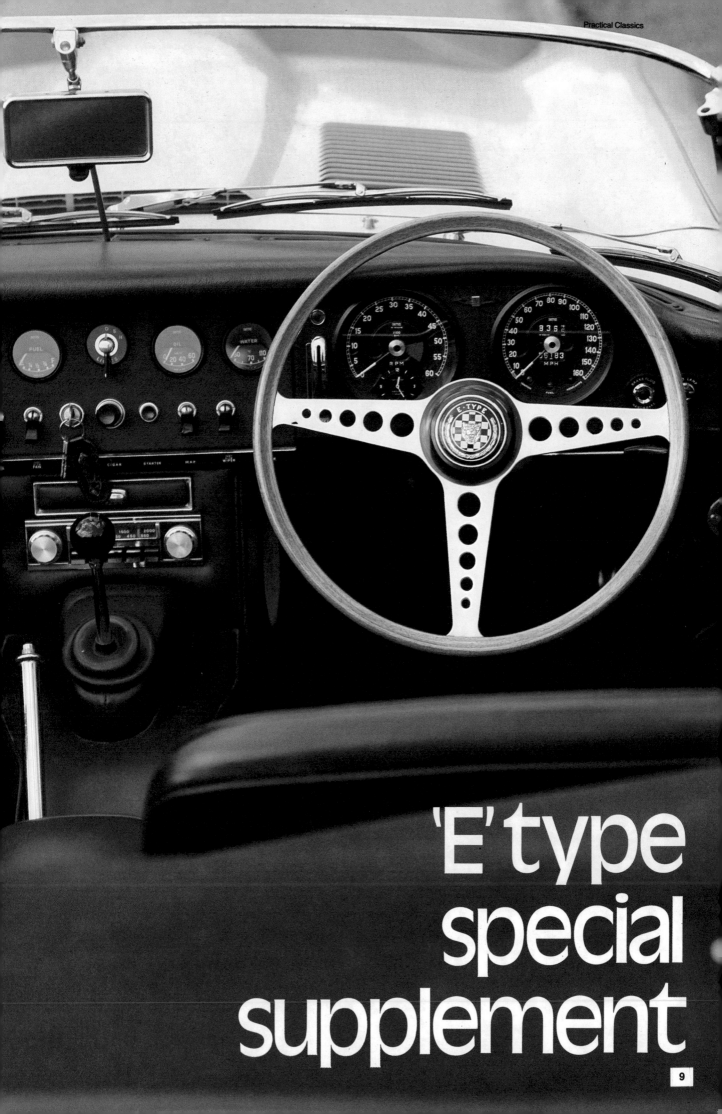

'E'type
special
supplement

'E' type!

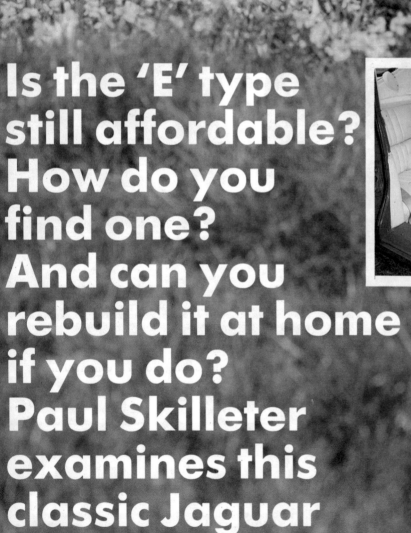

Is the 'E' type
still affordable?
How do you
find one?
And can you
rebuild it at home
if you do?
Paul Skilleter
examines this
classic Jaguar
from all angles...

A very long time ago I remember as a schoolboy gazing at a brand new, gleaming Jaguar 'E' type in a showroom window and thinking to myself that I just could not conceive of such a supremely beautiful machine ever becoming old. It seemed impossible that such lustrous red paintwork and sparkling chrome could ever be anything but perfect. Trying to imagine what an 'E' type would look like as a banger was like trying to imagine infinity – the mind simply couldn't grasp the concept.

It must have been fourteen years later that I was forcibly reminded of that moment in 1961. Driving to work through Islington in my company HC Viva I saw parked by the roadside an 'E' type roadster. It was red, just like the one I'd seen all that time before. But... the paintwork was dulled to a matt finish, the chrome was pockmarked with rust, the hood was faded and torn – and there was a great, gaping hole in the nearside sill. It had happened. The 'E' type had become an old car.

The writer's first 'E' type, 262 KOD; very much a 'used car' in the 1970s.

Left: Series 1 4.2 roadster (top); insets show 2-plus-2 interior, fixedhead luggage area, the triple carb. XK engine (derived from the XK 150S) and the very full 5.3 litre V12 engine bay of the Series 3 'E' type.

Not that the magic had disappeared; I'd had an XK for years but still the 'E' type's sensational looks exerted a strong appeal and, moreover, so did the promise of 150 mph performance and a real degree of comfort. Within a year I'd bought one, an early 3.8 fixed-head (the 246th rhd built) registered KOD 262 and finished in original, unresprayed metallic grey. I think it cost £1,700 – which was a lot of money in 1976 – but then it was so original, so rust-free and so straight that I didn't begrudge a penny of it. When I went freelance soon after KOD became an everyday, go-to-work car used in all weathers and, after sweltering in the baking summer of '76 we drove through the frosts and snows of winter. You get to know a car when you use it like that, in a way you never can when it's just a week-end toy.

Which 'E' type?

Seven or eight years have passed since I sold KOD to a young accountant in Slough, and things have changed a bit since; it was about that long ago (1982) that we last examined buying an 'E' type for restoration in *Practical Classics*. We said then that you didn't get much for under a thousand. Well, make that at least £15,000 if you're talking about a righthand drive 3.8 roadster – but if you settle for a fixed-head, like we've just done for our next Project Car, then you can still get in on the act for the price of a tatty TR6 because £5,000 – £7,000 will buy you a restoration-project Series 2 fixedhead, or a two-plus-two. In fact it's just possible to get a running, MoT'd Series 2 two-plus-two for not much

The most valuable of all 'E' types today (apart from competition ones) are the original 3.8 litre roadsters – especially if, like this export version with the rare hardtop, they have external bonnet catches and flat floors.

more than the last figure; it'll still need rebuilding, but you'll be able to get a few months' motoring out of it first.

The point of saying all this is that your choice of 'E' type is governed mainly by your wallet. Unless you make a freak purchase, open 'E's are out unless you've got upwards of £12,000 to spend (that'll buy you an incomplete left-hooker with the wrong or a missing engine), closed-headlight fixed-heads will cost you from £5,000 to £10,000, and two-plus-twos a little less. Series 3 V12

The 4.2 'E' had more torque and an alternator but the polished alloy cam covers were retained. The braking system was much improved too (on this lhd car the reserviours are on the nearside). Cross-ply tyres were generally fitted until 1964.

roadsters are something else again and you are unlikely to get even the rawest of raw material for less than £15,000-£20,000 – they've been dragged up by rocketing Ferrari prices. V12 fixed-heads are very affordable though, at £9,000 – £12,000. However, that won't be for long though, as more and more get converted to roadsters, a fate which will be encouraged by the appearance of new bodyshells from Martin Robey.

But don't dismiss the closed six-cylinder cars. To my mind a closed-headlamp fixed-head is even prettier than a roadster and, with the numbers being broken or converted into open cars, a good closed 'E' type (especially a 3.8) is going to have a distinct rarity appeal in a few years' time. The two-plus-twos don't have quite the same grace but have the great virtues of being more affordable – *and* you can put the kids in the back and go off for a weekend.

I also rate the closed car as being the more practical long distance, high speed tourer; even with the hood up the open cars are noisy and tiring. Then thanks to the rear door you can also carry six-foot long loads in the fixed-head. But I don't suppose people care about the sorts of practicalities that appealed to us everyday drivers a few years ago.

You also have to differentiate between 3.8

and 4.2, closed headlamp and open headlamp cars in the pecking order. The most valuable six-cylinder 'E' types are 3.8 roadsters, with a premium on the so-called 'flat floor' cars' with no footwells (Jaguar put them in shortly after launch to make the cars more driveable). Side bonnet catches are of snob value too. The 4.2 engine arrived during 1964 together with a completely revised interior which said goodbye to the appealing (though uncomfortable for some) bucket seats. Now called the 'Series 1' 4.2, this car wasn't much faster than the 3.8 but was blessed with Jaguar's new all-synchromesh gearbox. A good Series 1 4.2 fetches almost as much as a similar condition 3.8.

Then towards the end of 1967 came the variant now dubbed the 'Series 1½'; this was basically a Series 1 4.2 but without the light-scattering headlight covers. The full Series 2 arrived in 1968 in time for US safety/emission regulations and while UK-spec. cars lost no power from the same triple-carb. 4.2 engine, a larger air-intake, bigger front and rear sidelights and repositioned (open) headlights took the edge off the 'E' type's pure lines. The interior was modernised too with new switchgear, recessed door handles and so on. Cars for North America got twin Stromberg carbs. and a severely reduced performance – they were pushed to exceed 135 mph. The long wheelbase two-plus-two which had come along in 1966 received the same sort of attention.

The next set of changes were much more drastic and were centred around the two-plus-two long wheelbase car which was given Jaguar's new 5.3 litre V12 engine. There were all sorts of other alterations such as a new bonnet with flared wheel arches hiding a wider frame carrying the all-alloy power unit. The rear wheel arches were flared too and of course the interior was heavily revised. Roadster and fixedhead versions were available, the latter only featuring rear seats because of fears about open-car legislation in the United States. You could specify an automatic gearbox even in the roadster

This is a Series 2 dash; compare it with that of the Series 1 4.2 shown on the Supplement cover – rocker instead of flick switches and revised choke and heater controls are among the differences.

The V12 Series 3 fixedhead; although more bulbous, the lines are still graceful.

now, thanks to the extra room created by the longer wheelbase; it was all part of the 'E' type's new, softened character.

Whether you like the Series 3's looks is up to you, but don't ignore the car's thirst (around 13 mpg as opposed to 16-20 mpg of the six-cylinder). The fixedhead is currently one of the most affordable of all 'E' types but this won't last for long as they are increasingly being converted into roadsters. In fact, just as has happened to vintage Bentleys, closed V12 'E' types may one day be much rarer than open ones!

rocking with the engine's firing impulses, the car is now alive!

With the slab-like clutch pedal pushed fully down you ease the stubby gearlever into first. If there's a resistance or a grating sound – no synchromesh on first don't forget! – go back to neutral, release the clutch, blip the throttle and (important this) after waiting for the engine revs to die right back to tickover try again.

Now you can move off, the clutch smooth in its take up. As you accelerate you're immediately aware of the power that lies beneath your right foot – and of the typical Moss box whine. Move the lever back into second and I bet that first time round you'll either elicit a grating noise or not engage the new gear at all. If you're used to modern flick-switch gearboxes you'll find the old Moss-designed four-speeder slow and requiring practice; the technique is to knock it free of first then pause briefly in neutral before *easing* the lever into second.

Into third – a little notchy but not difficult to find – and you flex your right foot. The nose lifts and suddenly you're doing seventy, eighty, ninety. A quick movement and you're in top; in fact, third to fourth and back again is child's play and as you don't often need any other gear, these factors minimise the drawbacks of the anachronistic Moss device.

Now you're doing maybe 110 mph. Put your foot down, hard. Yes, the nose lifts again, the rear tyres dig in, and amidst a quiet surge of straight-six power the clear, black-faced speedo is showing 120 mph within seconds. Only when it reaches 130 does the

Driving and living with the legend

Presumably your basic aim in looking for an 'E' type to restore is to end up driving one around. What's it like being behind the wheel? Let's start with the 3.8.

The first thing you notice on climbing in is how low you sit in the delicate, thinly upholstered bucket seats and how the car, with those big high sills, encloses itself around you. The next thing you notice is the huge steering wheel, and then looking out over that, the length of the bonnet, dropping away out of sight. You've probably never sat in one, but it's all very reminiscent of the sports-racing 'D' type from which the car sprang.

You turn the key and press the polished black plastic starter button. There's a metallic ring as the starter pinion impinges on the flywheel and then the engine fires with a 'thrummm' that discreetly reverberates through the body; gently but perceptibly

The Series 3 roadster, its flared wheelarches clearly visible in this photograph. The last 50 'E' types, sold during 1975, were finished in black, except for the penultimate car which was green to special order.

acceleration noticeably tail off, but given a straight road and no speed limit, you should eventually see the needle nudge 147 mph or so, maybe 150 mph or more on a good day, one-way.

At these speeds you hardly hear the hum of the engine as wind noise has taken over, but the car feels solid and safe. Which is why, even if you never see such three-figure speeds in reality, the 'E' type feels so secure at more normal rates of progress. For the record, I used to find that the car felt a little busy at 90 mph but that it found a sort of second wind at 110 mph; 120 mph was its comfortable cruising speed, which anyway is as fast as you want to go in the vicinity of traffic and without having to concentrate to a tiring degree.

Corners? No worry, although the car prefers medium to fast speed bends. Sharper bends, that is those taken at below 70 mph, seem to highlight the narrowness of 185 section tyres and you are very conscious of that great heavy engine up front trying to push the nose wide. In these circumstances you need to set the car up for the apex to overcome the understeer and power round, allowing that marvellous rear suspension to bite and put the power down in the way it does so superlatively.

Rain or snow? If you've been told that the 'E' type is a handful in the wet, forget it – I've driven the car in all weathers and in all conditions and I've never felt safer in another car. With a progressive, long-travel throttle controlling a smooth, wide torque band you can feed in just as much, or as little, power as *you* want in any given situation and, unless you're totally stupid in first or second gear, you simply won't unstick the tail.

Braking on the 3.8 is less satisfactory. I never had full confidence in KOD's stopping department and encountered severe rear-brake fade on several occasions, to the extent that I really didn't think I was going to stop. It is tempting to blame the vacuum/mechnical servo (all the rest of the braking system was new on my car) but I just don't know. Some people are happy with the 3.8's brakes; quite a lot aren't. But they're fine for all normal purposes.

Ergonomically the 'E' type is an old car but I found you got used to the row of identical switches controlling minor functions such as the wipers from the central dashboard (alloy finished on early cars). My early fixedhead didn't have a heated rear window so I carried a stick-mounted windscreen scraper to clear condensation from the driving seat (when stationary, I hasten to add). Perhaps the car performed least satisfactorily in fog or mist as the closed headlights scattered the beam so badly you had to slow to a crawl. Then if you were stuck in traffic too, and had the heater motor and wipers on as well, you could (and I did) end up with a flat battery – the dynamo simply couldn't keep up. Yes, the car did leak a little in really wet weather but not as badly as some.

A well-maintained 'E' type that isn't worn out should be reliable. KOD was remarkably so; over many thousands of miles I was sidelined only twice, I think, once with a col-

Driving the 'E' type – still an exhiliarating experience today.

lapsed rear hub bearing and once with a failed control box. Otherwise the car just went on and on. A poor car can be a misery though, no matter how bright its paintwork.

The 'E' type retained the same broad handling and performance characteristics over the 4.2, Series 1½ and 2 model changes, though with their all-synchromesh gearboxes, alternators, better switch-gear and wider and (possibly) more comfortable seats they are more practical conveyances. The open headlights were a big step forward in practical terms too, even if they lost a few mph off the top speed. But the cars otherwise feel much the same and I did a good few miles in the factory's yellow Series 1½ roadster in the late sixties; in fact it was JDU 877E that gave me my first true contact with the breed – and hooked me for life.

It's with the Series 3 that you have to think differently. To be sure it's even more usable in terms of a few additional modern refinements but otherwise, though the V12 engine produces a gloriously smooth, unstrained surge of power, the Series 3 is softer and floppier than its predecessors, with the power steering taking the edge off its controllability and sportiness. But then to many, the appeal of twelve cylinders and a degree of extra comfort more than compensate for the Series 3's loss in clarity of performance and styling.

Whatever sort of 'E' type you are lucky enough to end up with though, you will never be bored and you'll always be aware that you possess one of the most enduringly beautiful – and fastest – British sports cars of all time.

This Series 1½ roadster was a factory press car and first introduced Paul Skilleter to 'E' types back in 1968.

Buying an 'E' type

Where to buy and what to look for

Yes – this imported roadster looks mega-rough, and so it is, but people are scrambling for such cars...

...even with the floors entirely rotted away. But the availability of new shells makes such details irrelevant.

The engine may be seized or dismantled but at least check that it carries the correct number – or at least an 'E' type number – on cylinder block and cylinder head. The block should have the cast '3.8' or '4.2' on the side and watch for cracks in the water jacket – this one has gone badly.

Okay, so you've decided to go for it. Where do you start? The first and most obvious source is the motoring press – *Practical Classics* might well turn up an 'E' type for restoration in the classified columns, but you'll need to cast your net wider and look in all the monthlies for a while. The first ads. you'll spot will probably be dealers and, certainly in the case of 4.2 and 3.8 roadsters, most of the cars they'll be advertising will have come from North America. BUT – you pay for the privilege of buying 'off the shelf' like this, and there are other dangers too.

Especially at the lower end of the price range you may be offered an incomplete car, for example a bare, rusty 'tub', and the danger here is that it's been imported as a part rather than a car. This means that even if you rebuild it to totally original condition, you may very well not be able to register it as a Jaguar – the registration authorities will say it doesn't exist. Or, if you manage to convince them that it is a Jaguar with a correct chassis number, you could end up with a 'Q' plate or another sort of inappropriate registration number. This will tend to spoil the final affect and will definitely reduce the car's value.

So lesson number one when buying an imported car is to check that it has the correct customs clearance form as a *car*. Next, check the engine and gearbox numbers against the chassis number to see if they all match up; an 'E' type without its original engine and other major units is not exactly a disaster but will have a reduced value and appeal when rebuilt. If you quote all the numbers to Jaguar they will tell you if they match up (but it's no good just sending in the chassis

number and ask what the original engine and gearbox numbers are – they may very well not tell you, in case you're trying to 'create' a car out of a few rusty bits). Write to the chassis records office, Jaguar Cars Ltd, Browns Lane, Allesley, Coventry – and allow several weeks for a response.

Now look around the car to see what else is missing; yes, a vast amount of stuff has been remanufactured but not everything, and you can spend a great deal of time and money hunting for oddments. However, you may have to accept this if you want to get onto the 'E' type ladder right at the bottom. At least you've bought your car at today's price, which will be half tomorrow's...which is also

why you won't find vendors willing to budge much on price. They know that they've only to keep the car for another six months and they'll get 30% more (dealers don't usually do this because they get their profit from turnover, importing maybe six cars at a time and selling them relatively quickly).

Supplies of 'E' types from the good old US aren't infinite though, and over the past few months values over there have rapidly climbed to match those here, at least so far as open six-cylinder 'rebuild-project' cars are concerned (good or rebuilt 'E' types are still

Fixedheads for restoration are becoming hard to find now, but occasionally you may come across an unfinished rebuild you can snap up.

heaper in the States). That's because American enthusiasts are waking up to the 'E' type as an investment too. Probably we're in the last few months of even vaguely affordable wrecks being brought into the UK from North America.

Fixed-head 'E' types are coming back too and it may occur to you to acquire a roadster identity in the form of a bare but useless tub and then cannabalise a closed car for mechanical bits to go on a Robey open bodyshell.

We're not going to discuss the ethics of such an operation – it has happened and it is going to happen in an ever-increasing number of cases, and it may well be the only affordable way to end up with an 'E' roadster. Or, you can simply 'chop' a fixedhead into a roadster; all the bits are now available to do so. It's up to you...but an open two-seater with a fixedhead chassis number will never be worth as much as the genuine thing, no matter how well it's been rebuilt.

If you're lucky, loose seats and trim will enable you to expose the rear bulkhead, which looks like this. It's divided up into compartments inside, and as in this 2-plus-2 was sometimes stuffed with moisture-retaining sound deadening material. Poke around especially where bulkhead meets floor and sill, and examine the rear wheel arches at the same time.

Assessing the prospect

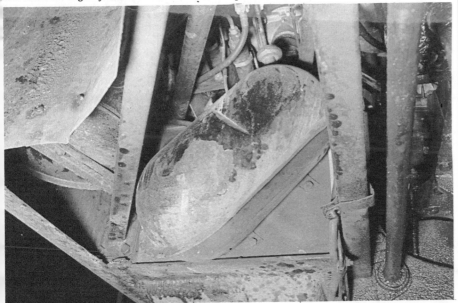

New shells have revolutionised the 'E' type restoration scene. These two, minus most of their outer panels, are awaiting collection at Martin Robey Engineering Ltd.

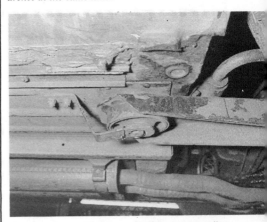

From underneath, the rear bulkhead looks like this – yes, it also carries the rear suspension's radius arm. Bulkhead floor frequently rots through.

To avoid unintentionally buying a car that needs a shell change, key points to examine are the bulkheads (indeed you may want to utilise the front bulkhead on an exchange basis anyway). This is a front bulkhead viewed from the front; note where the engine frame attaches at the outer bottom, a favourite point for serious rot – though even good bulkheads may need some repairs. Frame too must be carefully examined. Also visible on this shot of 262 KOD taken some years ago are the vacuum tank and (right) a front suspension torsion bar.

There is one major decision to be made when it comes to assessing a roadster for restoration: to re-shell or not to re-shell. The very fact that there's a decision to be made is thanks first and foremost to Martin Robey Engineering Ltd who pioneered the remanufacture of 'E' type bodyshells (although several other companies may now offer a similar service on a smaller scale). This option, which has just become available on V12 roadsters too, has transformed the 'E' type restoration scene, because even write-offs are now rebuildable. In fact, as hinted at earlier, it's getting to the point where all you'll need is an *identity* and any remains of the car itself will be of incidental interest only...

Professional restorers like the new shell system because it cuts out labour time and amateurs like it because it means that they can restore an 'E' type without having to possess 'A' level welding skills. The ideal subject for a shell-change is of course a very complete and original car but with a totally shot centre-section. Hard to find...

The key to buying a shell-change prospect is to do so intentionally. Plenty of people pay a lot more for a running car in a considerably higher price bracket only to find a bit later on that it is only really masquerading as just that. The photographs show you how to

assess an 'E' type bodily but, in brief, a shell-change job is more or less assured if the rot has destroyed a lot of the front and rear bulkheads. If these are sound, then dedication, time and a reasonable amount of skill will enable the car to be 'brought back', thanks to the availability of complete new sections, panels and repair panels.

The latter approach is what we're going to adopt on our *Practical Classics* Project Car 'E' type and in forthcoming months you'll have the advantage of Colin Ford showing you every step of its restoration. In fact, as you can't get new fixedhead shells yet, that's the technique you'll have to adopt for a closed car anyway. This calls for a more critical examination of the shell because you're commited to repairing it. Avoid a car where the rust has reached up to the rear side windows and up the windscreen pillar – unless you are very brave, that is.

Adjacent to the door pillar you may find that the Hopeful Bodger has been at work!

Rear wheel arches on fixedheads are particularly vunerable because of the sandwich join with the inner wing which is lacking on open cars.

A bonnet with this degree of corrosion in the vital wing/centre section flanges is most definitely a write-off!

A little bit of prodding of the outer sills will almost invariably reveal this sort of rust damage, extending right into the diaphragm plates, the inner sills and often the floor.

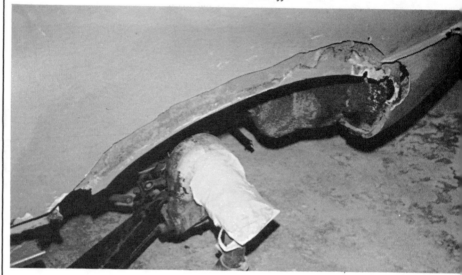

The engine frame needs a careful examination and if there is any doubt about its condition, budget for a new one – the youngest six-cylinder 'E' types are now 18 years old and the beautifully made but thin-walled Reynolds tubing can, with the passing of years and accident damage, rust and crack.

The bonnet represents a large part of an 'E' type; they are still available new and many restorers fit one automatically. But the amateur with more time on his hands may still find it practical to repair an original provided it hasn't deteriorated too far (i.e. along the wing/centre section seams in particular). We covered this work in *Practical Classics* not so long ago, in the July and August 1988 issues (see the Back Numbers page)

A final emphasis on searching out bodywork bodges: no vendor of a rebuild project should object to a bit of prodding in the car's vitals with a screw-driver, or pulling bits of trim out of the way to look at bulkheads etc. Better to be disappointed before you purchase than afterwards.

When it comes to the mechanical parts it's a distinct bonus if the car is running or even mobile; you can then get an idea of the condition of the gearbox and rear axle, possibly the suspension even. But we're talking here of buying for restoration so the chances are that

the best you'll be able to do is determine whether the engine is seized and that the suspension is at least complete. Take stories of how "the engine was completely rebuilt three years ago" with a large pinch of salt unless all the bills are to hand – and unless the engine has obviously been well protected during storage in the meantime.

What you must do is calculate the costs involved in the mechanical renovation – it's easy to to talk about new shells or whatever but forget that collectively, restoring the engine, transmission and suspension can

A visual check will probably have to suffice for the suspension; remember that just the parts for rebuilding the twin coil spring/damper rear suspension will run well into four figures.

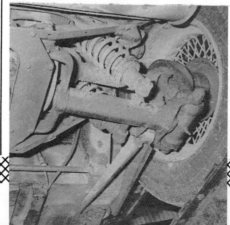

work out at a similar cost. For instance, extra jobs you hadn't bargained for may crop up, like the cylinder head needing to be welded-up due to corrosion of the aluminium. Parts for a six-cylinder XK engine full overhaul may come to £2,000 or even more depending on the condition of the unit and likewise, just the parts for a rear suspension rebuild will be well into four figures – as will a new braking system. It all adds up…

Similar calculations need to be made if you're anticipating getting professional help. Ask recognised specialists for estimates at an early stage so you can budget accordingly. A full restoration to new condition will cost around £30,000 for a six-cylinder car and you can work down from that according to how much you let the professional do. Get several quotes, try and visit the workshops yourself to see the standard of work, speak if possible to previous customers, and be prepared to wait several months before your car can be taken in. □

Pages 52 and 53:
The E type range (from left to right clockwise), Series 1 4.2 fixed head coupe, Series 1 roadster, Series 1 2+2 and Seies 3 V12 roadster. Our thanks go to the owners – Colin Ford, Russell Smith, Howard Tingey and Peter Werwood.

SPD 620 L

'E' type ...who does what.

The specialists

The 'E' type's massive popularity has created a whole industry and there are now many firms which either supply parts for, or rebuild, 'E' types. Most of the suppliers concentrate on new parts but a number also deal in used spares. Few 'E' types are scrapped these days but besides cars, large quantities of used parts have been arriving from the US in containers during the last few years and this means that it is still possible to find some of the spares that are not yet being remade. Our guess is, however, that this situation isn't going to last very long and if you're in need of a gearbox or engine block, you'd better secure them now!

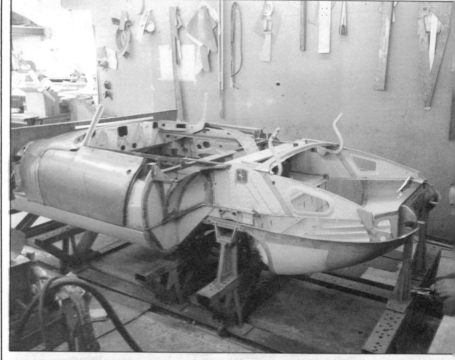

Jaguar, through Unipart, still offer some new 'ex-factory' parts for 'E' types especially on the mechanical front – wearing components for engines, for example. Bonnets are still marketed by Unipart (but as they're made in batches, don't calculate on being able to obtain one instantly) though hundreds of items have gone out of stock and it's fallen to independent specialists to reproduce them.

(Right): *top: a floor and bulkhead panels coming together on a jig at Martin Robey's to form a monocoque. Centre: RS Panels of Nuneaton also produce new 'E' type bodyshells to a very high standard. Bottom: Martin Robey also offers complete 'E' type bodies, with bonnet, if required.*

It won't surprise Jaguar enthusiasts if we begin with Martin Robey Engineering in this context. This Nuneaton firm has been in the 'E' type parts business longer than most and their capital investment in re-manufacture has been impressive. The firm even has its own press for making panels in house, though some are still hand-formed by wheeling machine. The latest enterprise is the remanufacture of Series 3 roadster shells, plus conversion kits for turning Series 3 fixedheads into roadsters.

Robey's bodyshells come in four distinct phases, all commencing with the basic sub-assembly which comprises the structural part of the car, jig assembled around either a new or reconditioned front bulkhead. The sub-assembly costs £2050 not including a new bulkhead (which adds £950). The professional or the experienced DIY-er can then panel-up this sub-assembly using either one of three panel kits; the cheaper 'Alpha' kit costing £623.75 contains the major outer panels but lacks such things as doors and bootlid. The 'Beta' kit includes these and costs £1173.75, while if you want a bonnet too, the ultimate is the 'Delta' kit which comes for £2454.75, this price being geared to the current Unipart bonnet price of £1281. All these prices are plus-VAT by the way.

All this is good as it allows the budget-conscious restorer to carry out at least some panel fitting and finishing, saving labour costs and, if appropriate, using repaired or second-hand doors, bootlid and bonnet. Most importantly, delivery times have been cut thanks to these part-complete sub-assemblies being much quicker to build than 100%, lead-loaded and finished bodyshells – but such is the interest in restoring 'E' types that you'd better get your order in some months in advance of when you think you'll need your sub-assembly.

Tooling-up for these shells has meant the re-introduction of many panels and detail parts which haven't been available for years, and most of these are offered seperately – great for the home repairer. This now applies to the Series 3 and the V12 boot floor which is just one item that has come on stream this year from Martin Robey thanks to the new bodyshell programme. But as Martin Robey himself would be quick to point out, his firm offer far more than 'just' panels – a huge range of mechanical, trim and brightwork items are stocked, from new heater boxes to new rear lights. Martin Robey Engineering can be contacted on 0203 386903/329112.

Other firms produce new bodyshells too, though Bob Smith's world-renowned **RS Panels** (also of Nuneaton, tel: 0203 388572) perhaps now tends to produce them more for special purpose cars such as competitive 'E' type replicas than for every-day rebuilds. But a valuable source providing impeccable workmanship nonetheless.

Going back to basics though, for unavailable original spares **R.M. & J. Smith** (in Crew, Cheshire, phone 0270 666608) are hard to match, Richard Smith having been one of the leading importers of North American 'E' types and parts over the past few years

It's not always essential to resort to a new shell, and while such work is not for the beginner, even badly rotted shells can be recovered by the traditional process of cutting and welding. This is a 2-plus-2 under renovation at Southern Classics.

types now, at least at affordable money. Another major importer is Steve Barrett of **S.N.G. Barrett** (tel: 0902 892307) and he also holds a large range of new 'E' type parts. **Jeremy Broad** (0836 509861) is also worth contacting in your search for an 'E' type to restore.

Retailers who can be relied upon for a good all-round parts service for 'E' types include **S.C. Jaguar Components Ltd,** Heritage approved and who operate a highly sophisticated spares business from Crawley (tel: 0293 547841), **ISP** (International Spare Parts Ltd) who sell cars for rebuild and new parts (tel: 01 450 0488/9), **Norman Motors** (one of the oldest names in the business – tel: 01 431 0940), and **Classic Spares of Enfield** – Martin Pike recently expanded the business to include full 'E' type rebuilds while remaining a stockist for Robey panels and many other parts (tel: 01 805 5534).

David Manners (tel: 021 544 4040) and **FB Components** (0865 724646) are very established names in the parts game, while **A.A. McInnes** are well-known for their

engine rebuilding and carb. reconditioning services (tel: 0274 531377), as is **Forward Engineering** whose speciality is also performance modifications (tel: 0676 23526); then **Southern Classics** have long been noted for their restorations of XKs and latterly 'E' types (tel: 0932 567671). **Lionheart Engineering** (tel: 0455 213063) has recently been set up by Richard Beaty, son of the Forward Engineering Ron Beaty; he specialises in engine rebuilds. **Barry Hatton International** (tel: 021 353 1013) supplies electrical components, and the **British Sports Car Centre's** Jaguar Shop is very strong in parts for 'E' types of every description (tel: 01 748 7824). **SMS Accessories** (tel: 01 391 1583) supply chrome dashpot covers for SUs and have other items applicable to 'E' types too. **Moor Wheel Services** have been linked with 'E' types for many years as they manufacture the wire wheels often fitted to the cars. These they can supply in various finishes including chrome, and (if you want extra tyre widths) in different rim sizes and offsets. Telephone 061 428 7773 or 0753 49360 for more details. **Lynx Cars** of St Leonards, Sussex are justly famous for their superb 'D' type replicas (based on 'E' type identities incidentally) but it shouldn't be overlooked that they offer a variety of services as well, including inlet manifolds for fitting Weber carburettors to 'E' types. And an 'E' type engine bay resplendant with triple twin choke carbs, is a dramatic sight indeed.

Finally, we musn't forget to mention **CF Autos,** whose Colin Ford will be tackling our Project Car 'E' type soon. This may tie him up for a few months but it won't last for ever! His number is 0322 346584.

In short, the 'E' type restorer is spoilt for choice! □

INTRODUCING OUR
'E'type!

Sponsored by
CONDOR

PRACTICAL CLASSICS RESTORATION PROJECT

PART ONE

1 *Well, here it is – the Practical Classics 'E' type Project Car in all its glory. The bonnet is missing (it's scrap, actually) and the car is now finished in maroon – but with a dozen other colours showing through including a hideous green. We'll be finishing it in its original British Racing Green.*

2 *A check was made of all underbonnet components to assess which were missing; very few were as, indeed, Geof Maycock had promised. Even the little GRP cowl over the steering column where it meets the bulkhead was there.*

4 *This is called the 'picture frame' and is the rectangle of tubes at the front of the frame. The top crossmember on our car is remarkably free from damage often caused by clumsy engine removal. The bonnet-hinge mounting frame projecting from it is unusually straight too – it's often a victim of ignorant tyre fitters who try to jack the car up on it (which also pushes the radiator into the bonnet...).*

3 *Colin then homed in to one of the really critical points on an 'E' type – the bottom outer sub-frame mountings. On the nearside this lies under the battery (rhd cars) and spilt acid often exacerbates rust damage. Despite heavy blows from a sharp implement both bulkhead and tubing appeared surprisingly sound on our car.*
On V12s and lhd cars the offside frame mounting is the more vulnerable; this is, however, our car and it has suffered from a typically bad repair to the bulkhead.

5 *The bulkhead lip also suffers from hamfisted engine removal/replacement and it can rust, too, under the rubber, which needs to be peeled back for inspection. The lip on our car was, again, above average.*

Our 'E' type Jaguar project begins with an assessment of the raw material. Paul Skilleter and Colin Ford take a hard look at what exactly needs doing.

We ought to start the story with how we selected our particular E' type. The search began many months ago but, while we anticipated difficulties in finding the right car, we still under-estimated the task. Initially we'd intended getting a 3.8 roadster but it quickly became clear that right-hand-drive cars for restoration were as good as non-existent and that only left-hookers from the United States were to be had. And these at a price £12,000-£13,000 for what were often rusty, stripped tubs with only the chassis plate usable. Such is the current popularity of 'E' types... But if you want to try your luck, Richard Smith, Jeremy Broad and Steve Barrett are among the people you should contact.

So in the end we settled for an honest, home-market fixed-head, a 4.2 to boot but at least right-hand-drive and with (virtually) all its original parts. The year is 1968 and the car is one of the last 'Series 1' cars built, featuring the closed headlights. Visually the early 4.2 is almost identical to the 3.8 fixed-head – a lovely shape, perhaps even better-balanced than the roadster. Anyway, it's the vision of the finished car in all its glory that'll spur us on...

Colin Ford of CF Autos is carrying out the restoration at his one-man workshop in

PRACTICAL CLASSICS RESTORATION PROJEC

Erith, Kent. The car duly arrived on its trailer from Autocats of Rawreth, Essex (Autocats, if you remember, rebuilt our Mk 2 Jaguar), proprietor Geof Maycock having decided, slightly reluctantly, to sell us the car which he'd had for a couple of years; the money will be going into the purchase of Mk 2s to restore, this being Autocats' main line of business.

You can't afford to be *that* choosy when buying an 'E' type for restoration these days because (a) the ideal car probably doesn't exist and (b) while you're making up your mind, someone else will probably buy it – although you stand a better chance with a closed 'E' type, and, indeed, you can be quite selective when it comes to the 2-plus-2 which hasn't caught on to the same extent yet. Key points to watch in all cases are that the engine and gearbox numbers match those on the chassis plate because, while a different engine etc. is not a complete disaster, the more major original units the car retains the more highly it will be regarded when it's finished. If the car comes from abroad and is very incomplete, check that it's not been imported as parts (in which case you could have troubled registering it when you're restored it). Also important is the general completeness of the car; while many items have been remanufactured, not everything has. It's not so much that you can't eventually find secondhand replacements, just the great amount of time and expensive 'phone calls you'll be in for tracking the stuff down. Judging completeness is extra difficult when a car has been totally dismantled and you should try to get the price reduced accordingly – you are *bound* to find bits missing later on.

The examination

Our car arrived partially stripped and this was a help when buying the car, as we could get a better look at the floors and rear bulkhead with the seats and carpets out. They didn't seem too bad either – but we must start at the beginning, with the engine frame.

Almost uniquely, Jaguar combined a monocoque shell with a tubular space frame when they designed the 'E' type, a method of construction carried over from the sports-racing 'D' type of the fifties. This frame carries the bonnet hinge mountings, the front suspension and the engine so it has quite a lot to do. This makes it imperative that it is in good condition, and the special Reynolds tubing is not immune to rust or accident damage. So we gave the frame a close examination – and found it surprisingly good. Had cracking (usually due to internal rusting) or deep corrosion been found we would have resolved to replace the frame as it's a safety-related item and short cuts are not a good idea.

A note was made at this time of the under-bonnet components generally; these were very complete and in reasonable condition, even the heater box which often rots out from underneath.

As for the bodyshell, the photographs take you through our probings of that, although until every bit of paint has been removed it's

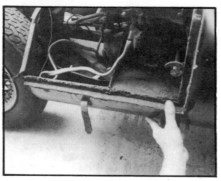

6 *A complete suspension strip will follow in due course so we just gave the area a quick visual look-over; everything appeared to be there and the splined hubs seemed relatively unworn. Odd wheels were fitted though, 'curly-hub' one side and straight the other!*

7 *Clumsy gas-welding in place of Jaguar's neat spot-welding instantly gave away the nearside sill replacement job; the bulkhead itself in this area doesn't seem too bad though from inside the car our probing screwdriver did find some rot. The footwells give food for thought – they're almost repairable but it's still tempting to fit new.*

8 *Obviously trouble brewing here! Door shut plate has disintegrated where it meets the sill and, chiselling away at where the rear wing joins, we found a massive depth of filler – but (apparently) covering up accident damage rather than rot.*

9 *The same area viewed from inside the car: note repairs to the inner sill (right), though floor and bulkhead appear reasonable. But further cleaning-off will probably reveal pin-holing at the very least; a good omen so far, though.*

10 *More filler but surprisingly few holes – that sums up our 'E' type's rear end. But we fully expect to find more rust damage on removing the tank and stripping the metal of filler and paint completely.*

The condition of the metal hidden by the fuel filler cap shouldn't be forgotten – a blocked drain hole often leads to rust in the rear corner of the filler aperture.

not possible to be absolutely catagoric about the extent of rot present. It is always possible for example, that the front bulkhead has rusted all the way up (and corrosion can spread right on to the horizontal parts and into the windscreen pillar areas). Overall, we concluded that our 'E' type is a real mixture and a bit of a surprise – as Colin says, because if 'X' has rusted you would normally expect that 'Y' would be too but, with our car, it often isn't; and *vice versa* – the legendary curate's egg, in fact.

ACTICAL CLASSICS RESTORATION PROJECT

'E'type!

What emerged from our initial inspection of the shell, therefore, is that the re-silling of the nearside might well have been because of accident damage rather than catastrophic rust because both front and rear bulkheads are above average in this respect and so are the floor pans. Whether the wrinkles in the roof are connected with this supposed accident is unknown but they certainly caused the roof to be covered in vinyl at some stage to disguise the problem. Colin said he felt much better once he'd torn that vinyl roof off – you can see him enjoying it in the heading picture!

He is now debating whether the roof is repairable (and it's a terrible place to try to eradicate dents, because the smooth reflective surface at just about at eye-level shows no mercy if you get it wrong…). If not, then the still-intimidating task of replacing the roof looms up; we've already contacted Lynx Engineering of St Leonards, Sussex (they carry out fixed-head to roadster conversions amongst much else), and earmarked a 'new' roof just in case.

The bonnet which came with the car Colin does not think is economically repairable, so we are getting a new one. For those who need to repair a bonnet, however, we have already covered this in *Practical Classics* and will indeed be returning to the topic of bonnets in general later on in this series.

The car we found to be complete with few vital interior or exterior pieces missing. The engine is original but has a badly cracked block; we're investigating the repair of this right now, and that will be covered in the engine overhaul section of this series later on. ☐

11 *Doors were checked for play; the nearside wasn't bad but the offside was dreadful and its door skin had almost completely rotted free from the frame.*

Next month
Stripping the car of its suspension – and further investigations into the condition of the shell.

PRACTICAL CLASSICS RESTORATION PROJECT

'E' type!

Sponsored by
CONDOR

Part 2

The mechanical strip-down of our 'E' type begins — Philip Cooper reports.

PRACTICAL CLASSICS RESTORATION PROJECT

'E' type!

In last month's issue, we introduced our latest restoration project – the 'E' type. A general assessment of the car was laid down along with a few points of interest that must be taken into careful consideration when buying such a vehicle. Although the engine, gearbox and exhaust have been removed, these are relatively straightforward procedures, adequately covered in any Jaguar or Haynes manual. LAY 394E now stands ready for its strip down and that is where we shall begin.

The starting point for this restoration is the removal of the rear axle and, with the car elevated, axle stands should be placed under the chassis rails.

The radius arm check strap may now be removed. This is held underneath by two bolts which locate up through the floor pan to the inside of the car. A third main bolt through the radius arm cap is usually wired. With the wire removed, the bolt should now be taken out, allowing the radius arm to drop.

To release the anti-roll bar as part of the next stage, it is possible to undo the mounting blocks that are held to the body, allowing the roll bar to be removed as a unit with the rear axle. However, due to restricted access and rusting on the metal bracket which secures the mount, it is usually easier to separate the anti-roll bar from the axle. The anti-roll bar may then be removed from the body once the axle has been dropped. Either way, it's advisable to remove the rear wheels before embarking on this task to gain a better access

Probably due to previous work carried out on the car, our differential had already been separated from the drive shaft. The next stage, therefore, is to disconnect the hand brake cable by removing the clevis pin and fully unscrewing the adjuster. During engine removal at an earlier stage, it had been necessary to take out the centre console. In doing this, the handbrake needed to be pulled to its fullest degree and, to facilitate such a movement, the handbrake cable had been disconnected; therefore this stage of the work also had been completed already.

Because the brake pipes are to be renewed it saves time to cut through these during axle removal. They may then be disconnected from the axle once it has been removed from the car. Care should be taken, of course, to catch any brake fluid that spills from the open pipes.

We strongly advise that, throughout the duration of the restoration, none of the components that are removed should be discarded, regardless of their condition. This even applies to cut pipes, or bolts that are rusted beyond use. Only when their counterpart has been sourced, mated up with the old unit and correctly installed on the car, should

12 *A trolley jack is essential and should be used with a block of wood which will spread the load more evenly over a larger area.*

13 *Due to rusting, it is probable that the radius arm will not drop down freely after the bolts have been removed and may necessitate the use of a crow bar, or even heat.*

15 *The far side of the forward-most rear axle mount is readily accessible.*

they be thrown away.

You should now check the position of the jack which should be a touch forward from the centre of the drive shafts. As the axle is rather heavy it is important to do this now so that the axle is correctly balanced for removal. On completion, the forward-most rear axle mounting bracket may be removed

14 *The bolt at the bottom of the drop link connection will separate the anti-roll bar from the axle.*

by undoing the two bolts which secure it to the body, noting any shims that are found here. Because it's not possible to gain access to the far side of the rear mount, as it is with the forward mount (except on series III roadsters and all 2 + 2s), it will be necessary to undo the three bolts which secure this mount to the axle, rather than the body, and remove the mount from the body once the axle has been removed.

Front suspension

Jacking up the front end of the car, placing axle stands under the lower bar of the picture frame and removing the front wheels, now enables us to concentrate on the front suspension.

There are several split pins located in the front suspension, many of which will be rusted to such a degree as to prevent removal. In such cases simply fit the socket and shear the pin in two.

It will be necessary to support the weight of the stub axle assembly with a jack placed under the lower ball joint cap before the shock absorber can be unbolted and removed. With this completed, the drop link should be disconnected from the front anti-

PRACTICAL CLASSICS RESTORATION PROJECT

The column may now be pulled back and away from the rack. The mounting brackets that secure the rack to the picture frame are held by two failsafes and one other bolt located on the opposite side of the picture frame verticals. Once removed, the failsafes must be retained and re-used as accurate replacements are particularly difficult to come by.

The top wishbone may now be removed. Several shims which set the camber are located with the rear mount and, if the same wishbones are to be replaced, it's advisable that these are kept to prevent lengthy camber adjustment procedures at a later date.

20   *Removing the top wishbone.*

16   *The axle removed, leaving the car on stands.*

roll bar, This bolt, however, was seized into its bush. It was therefore necessary to remove the drop link where it connected to the lower wishbone.

The nut that retains the tie rod end also caused problems by spinning the ball joint when turned rather than unwinding down the thread. To combat this it was necessary to exert a downward pressure on the ball joint, using the crow bar. The top wishbone ball joint presented the same problem. This was overcome by jacking the stub axle assembly further up and again employing the crow bar to force the ball joint down. After cutting the brake pipes which are to be replaced with new units, the lower ball joint is now undone and the whole front stub axle assembly may be removed.

As the mudguards are to be replaced, these can now be chiselled or cut off, thus giving improved access in these areas. The inboard locating bracket for the mudguard should also be removed along with the bolt below this which secures the inner shield; this will now be free to be taken out. Finally, the two uppermost bolts on the torsion bar shield are undone and, with the removal of a third bolt at its forward end, this may be pulled clear of the framework.

18   *Using an extractor on the lower ball joint.*

Before the steering rack can be removed it must first be disconnected from the column. Where the universal joint meets the steering rack there is an Allen screw that must be removed. To prevent this screw from rounding, thus causing problems, we strongly advise the use of Allen sockets. Failing this only use a high quality Allen key that will not break, lose its shoulders or round the screw.

19   *The failsafe that locates the steering rack mounting brackets to the picture frame.*

Remove the anti-roll bar by unbolting its brackets from the picture frame and proceed to the lower wishbone which, once removed, will conclude this month's strip-down. It is worth noting that the whole of the frame assembly can be removed and replaced complete depending on your choice, but it will require three or four people to help in doing this.

In next month's issue we intend to cover the removal of the front frames, then progress to the car's interior. In the meantime though, if you are restoring an 'E' type we suggest that you begin to list all the parts that you intend to replace and start making the necessary orders. This should be done as early as possible as there are long waiting lists for many parts which could cause considerable delays in your restoration timetable. ☐

Next month
Removal of the front frame and beginning to strip the car's interior.

17   *Using the crow bar on the top wishbone.*

Classic Car Insurance
With special rates for Jaguar Enthusiasts' Club members

OFF THE ROAD COVER

This scheme provides ACCIDENTAL DAMAGE, FIRE & THEFT cover for vehicles at all times except when they are being driven under their own power. It includes trailing and exhibition risks and damage whilst parked at an event or show and at a concours on display.

Cover of course applies whilst the vehicle is in its home garage so this cover is ideal whilst a vehicle is undergoing restoration in anticipation of future road risks.

COMPREHENSIVE COVER WITH AGREED VALUE

☐ This 'Classic Car Scheme' offers Full Comprehensive Cover, subject to a damage excess, with an AGREED VALUE basis for vehicles over 20 years of age, and will also cater for the more up-to-date models over 10 years of age.

☐ We recognise that vehicles purchased as collectors items or for investment are not normally used for everyday transport, and the premium level reflects limited usage, and no further laid up rebate is allowed.

☐ Only one road risk is charged provided the mileage limitation is not exceeded.

☐ **The premiums quoted are flat rate premiums, not subject to 'No claim bonus', and drivers must be club members and aged over 25 years of age.**

Mileage allowance available is 3,000, 5,000 or 7,000 per annum.

CLASSIC AND INVESTMENT CARS

☐ To cater for more unusual risks we have now also extended the scheme to cover HIGH VALUE VEHICLES.

☐ We have the capacity to arrange accidental damage up to £2,000,000 and cover for drivers of unusual occupations or normally too young to be eligible for the classic car scheme covered above.

☐ We will cover cars of any age, right up to the brand new car only taken delivery last week, again with discounts for Limited Mileage.

☐ We are willing to offer quotations on Individual Vehicles, Multi-Vehicles with a shared mileage, or Vehicles forming a collection.

☐ Vehicles should be garaged overnight and drivers must have access to another vehicle for their main use.

☐ All our policies can be extended for Wedding Hire, both professionally and for the occasional user. We can also offer a special package for members who work in the Motor Trade. Please contact our Motor Department direct for an individual quotation.

IF YOU DO NOT REQUIRE ONE OF OUR CLASSIC SCHEMES THEN WE CAN ALSO OFFER STANDARD MOTOR INSURANCE AT COMPETITIVE RATES WITH DISCOUNTS TO CLUB MEMBERS.

Wedding Hire Available

Windscreen Cover included

CLASSIC CAR FINANCE
We can now arrange finance at competitive rates to purchase the car of your dreams, or to complete that unfinished restoration project.
All enquiries treated in the strictest of confidence – Phone us now for further details.

CLASSIC CAR MOTOR POLICIES
For unbiased advice without obligation contact us
` at: CLASSIC HOUSE
365A LIMPSFIELD ROAD
WARLINGHAM, SURREY CR3 9HA
0883-627491/2/3/4/5

CLASSIC CAR MOTOR POLICIES ARE PART OF THE *CJH* GROUP OF COMPANIES

'E' type!

Sponsored by
CONDOR

Part 3
**Philip Cooper
reports as
Colin Ford's
work progresses
to the interior.**

PRACTICAL CLASSICS RESTORATION PROJEC

'E' type!

It should be realised from the start that such an in-depth restoration as this is going to take up a lot of space. Ideally you need to allow for a working and storage area to the sum of approximately three times the size of the car. Another point to note is that it's helpful to take plenty of photographs throughout the duration of such a project. This is particularly true in the more complicated areas such as the dash where illustrations of wiring connection and location may prove invaluable during the later rebuild stages.

As previously mentioned, it is Colin Ford who is leading us step by step through the 'E' type restoration. Colin, who restored his own '64 series I 3.8 fhc several years ago, has been running CF Autos, now at 5 South Road, Erith, Kent (Tel: 0322 346584), for over ten years, the majority of which have been dedicated to the preservation of 'E' types.

Turning our attention to LAY 394E, you will notice that the car is on a jig. Unfortunately this has to be done although earlier we stated to the contrary but, in this case, the accident damage leaves us with no alternative.

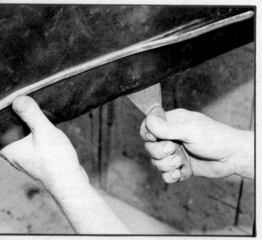

21 Insert a scraper and move around the edges, pulling outwards as you go to release the interior trim panel.

This month, we will progress as far as the removal of the front frames. As we will be going under the car now and in the future, it's as well to clean off any sealant, rustproofing or dirt etc. straight away to make work easier and cleaner. We've also removed the front windscreen.

To gain access to some of the bolts that secure the frame mounts it will be necessary to remove some sections from inside the car, so we may as well to take out the whole of the interior at this stage. With the doors out of the way, access in and out of the car will be greatly improved and so this is where we shall begin.

22 Remove the window winder and door handle by pushing its rim in towards the trim, then tap out the pin in the centre.

With the trim panel removed from the door, the four bolts and two screws that secure the hinge should be taken out. The highest of these four bolts is located under a slight lip and, if it is rusted, may require some patience to remove. However, if, as in our case, the doors are to be replaced, this lip can be bent upwards enabling the use of a socket. The chrome strip above the window winder should be removed at this point because, once the door has been taken off, if it has been left in place it will protrude beyond the end of the door and be susceptible to damage. The door will now slide outwards and, with its far end angled upwards, should come free. This will leave the hinge connected to the bodywork thus making the later stage of re-hanging a lot easier.

The horn-push on the steering wheel is secured by three grub screws located in the boss and therefore no attempt should be made simply to prise this off. The removal of this will reveal a locking nut and a main retaining nut. With these wound off, the steering wheel can be slid off its splines.

23 After the steering wheel has been taken off, these split cones will need to be removed and carefully stored.

If your model is fitted with a heated rea windscreen, then the wiring for this must b disconnected from underneath the rear doo trim panel. The door may now be taken of by unbolting the two hinges which agai should be left on the shell.

Removal of the rear quarterlight come next and, after unscrewing the inside hinge the five screws that are located on the rear ward side of the pillar should be undon

24 Gradually undoing the screws on the quarterlight B post will release the window. There's no need actually to remove these screws.

ACTICAL CLASSICS RESTORATION PROJECT

27 *The underside locating mount for the fuel tank should have a strengthening bracket, but it was not obvious that this was missing until the undersealant had been cleared away.*

25 *Undoing the screws in the cantrail. When any screw is found to be seized, it's often best to tighten slightly to crack any rust or seizure, making the screw easier to undo.*

In the corner of the dash on the right-hand side of the driver there is a chrome finish which must be unscrewed to reveal further screws which also need to be taken out. This releases the corner of the trim. Lifting the rear door catch enables you to unscrew its chrome surround. With the removal of the other screws that hold this trim panel from the inside, you should take out all the screws from the cantrail. These should be laid out on the roof in the correct order as some are longer than others and should not be incorrectly replaced. Unscrewing the seat belt anchorage will now allow the respective

26 *Scrape the foam off the wheelarch as close to the metal as possible.*

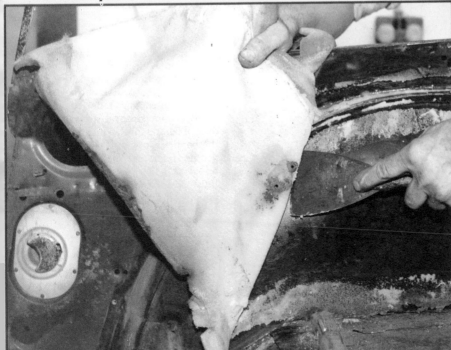

trims, that might be lightly glued, to be taken out. To remove the rear door seal, it is necessary to release the rear door catch slightly and the rear interior light.

Whether you decide to keep the interior wheelarch trims or not, particular care should be taken during removal to ensure that you scrape them off as closely to the metal as possible. A certain amount of foam will remain glued to the metal but the less the better as this has to be cleaned off at a later stage. Drill the rivets out of the vertical luggage compartment cross panel and the brackets behind it and take the panel out from behind the seats along with any carpet sections and soundproofing.

Before the petrol tank can be removed, it must first be drained. The drain plug is in the petrol tank sump tube located at the rear on the underside of the car. The sump tube should now be unscrewed and, moving back inside the car, the cover plate should be

unbolted and removed along with the filler to tank tube which is secured with two Jubilee clips. The tank itself is bolted to the car at three corners and underneath at the rear where the axle is usually located. With the tank now loosened we juggled it about to reveal the breather pipe which goes up into the filler neck. Disconnecting this and the wires from the sender unit allowed us to slide the tank out of the car.

Following this, we moved to the front of the car and removed the soundproofing from around the footwells. Also to come out were the bonnet release and the trim around it. Once the release has been unbolted from the far side of the bulkhead it can be disconnected and pulled through. The under-dash cowling was then unscrewed either side of the steering column and the trip meter and clock change were removed.

The steering column was our next subject for removal. We turned the boss to reveal the pinch bolts on the universal joint. Because the series I has an adjustable column we also had to undo the pivot bolts further up and either side of the column. This then dropped but, before it could be taken out of the car,

28 *The pivot bolts are bushed.*

the purple horn wire and all the bullet wires needed to be disconnected.

We now undid the dash top which was held in place by two screws in the fuse box and one screw at each of its ends. This gave us access to the wipers. The wiper motor is connected directly to the central wiper. To release it, we had to pull back the two flanges on the drive arm where the ball joint meets the wiper. The motor, which was located on the bulkhead, was now unbolted and removed. We then took off the speedometer cable but, before the dash could be fully removed, the two main looms that feed the rear of the car had to be disconnected and pulled through. There is, however, nothing to be gained by removing the small loom on the nearside that feeds the interior light, so we unplugged this from the main loom and left it in place.

We next removed the trim panel above the

PRACTICAL CLASSICS RESTORATION PROJECT

'E' type!

these should be secured by wing nuts. If on removal the jets appear to be in good condition, it's advisable to re-use them. This is because the replacement jets obtainable from various suppliers can be difficult to fit, again due to the restricted access in the bulkhead. Re-chroming of the old units is not really advisable unless you can source some spare ones from other Jaguar models on which they are common, as the success rate for good chroming can be fairly low.

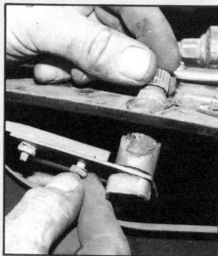

32 *Prising off the bonnet support frames.*

29 *Two of the bolts that secure the passenger side of the dash.*

30 *Removing the wiper through the body-work.*

passenger footwell which is held in by two screws. Then all the wires from the dials on the driver's side were disconnected and the screws and bolts that hold this section were taken out. The heater control cables were released and the two pivot bolts that hold the main fuse box section were removed. These bolts are bushed and care should be taken to retain the bushes. Disconnect any remaining electrical fixings and drop the centre section and all the wiring, thus completing the dash removal.

Before we unbolted the wipers, we sprayed them with WD 40. This is because the threads here are alloy and, if seized, will break or be ground off as a result of any effort to remove them. With the wipers unbolted, their cowls can be removed as should be the wiper park adjustment.

If you have particularly large hands, now is the time to butter up your wife or girlfriend and assure her that it won't be long before the car's finished (a little white lie never hurt) if she will only spend a few moments helping you. Once the riveted brackets that secure the heater, vacuum and air pipes to the front of the bulkhead have been drilled, the pipes will need to be taken out of the bulkhead box section. This is where problems may be encountered as access to this section is very limited and, even if you can get your hands in there, you still have to feel about, locate and extract the relevant pipes which is where the size of your lady friend's hands will be very advantageous.

With the wiper assembly out of the way, the washers will no longer be obstructed and should now be removed along with their respective piping. Provided the washer jets on your car haven't been replaced in the past,

We've again turned our attention to the final removal of the wipers. This time we disconnected the driver's side wiper from the drive rod in the same manner as the central unit was released. This procedure was then applied to the nearside wiper. Following this, we pulled down the central wiper through the body top and prised off the escutcheon. Moving the whole assembly to the left allowed us to bring the drive rod from the right-hand wiper through the central aperture in the bulkhead. It was then possible to pull the whole wiper assembly out of the bulkhead.

Before we could remove the pedal box, it was necessary for Colin to take off the pedals which, if left in place, would not fit through the hole above the driver's feet. With this done, and having removed the brake and clutch pipes and the accelerator cable, the pedal box was removed along with the glassfibre steering column cowl. Try to save the pedal box gasket – replacements are scarce.

31 *Removing the pedal box.*

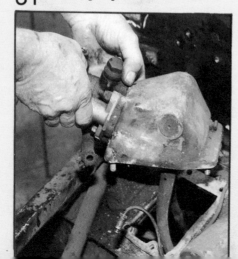

33 *It was necessary to apply heat to one of the frame's lower mounts which had seized in place.*

We've now come to the last stage in this issue – the removal of the frames, which is quite simple and very straightforward. We started by noting the course that the brake line takes along the frame. The junction was then unbolted and removed as were the horns. Frame removal is basically a procedure of bolt removal, which should start with the bonnet support frames. Then undo the picture frame, noting the shims that are found at the bottom joints. The remaining third and final section of the frame is unbolted from the car, starting at the bottom, and then releasing the uppermost mounts to complete the job.

Next month
Interior panel renewal and fixing, prior to sill replacement.

'E' type!

Sponsored by CONDOR

Part 4

Colin Fords attention turns to the bodywork while Philip Cooper reports the procedure.

PRACTICAL CL

'E' type!

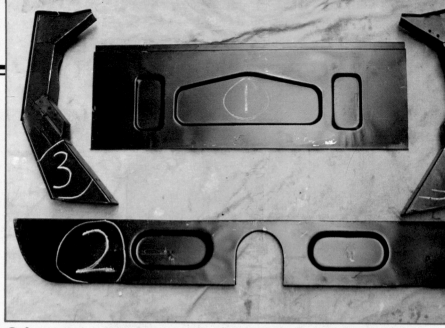

34 *The first of our replacement panels*

With our 'E' type adequately stripped of its internal and external fittings, we are now faced with a very sad looking car and ahead of us lies what I would have considered to be the grim reality of turning this carnage of metalwork in to a shape that represents its former elegance. On the other hand, for Colin, it is viewed as a mere formality of natural progression. In other words, for those of you carrying out a restoration, this is no time to become disheartened as the more systematical you are in tackling the body work repairs the easier it will be.

For reasons previously mentioned, our car is on a jig and it is obviously at this stage that this may prove to be crucial. However, many home restorations of this type have been successfully completed without jigs and, provided you take due care, then satisfactory results should be obtained. If your project car has a fixed head, then the task will be easier than that of completing a drophead. Whichever the case, the more precautions you employ the greater your chances of a successful re-build. By this we suggest that you tackle one job and one side at a time, only progressing to the next job when the previous work is finished and welded up. In this way you will maintain as much rigidity in the body at any one time as possible, thus minimising the chances of bodily distortion leading to incorrect panel fitment. To the same end, you should refer to, and continuously check, as much data on the car as you can possibly glean from workshop manuals etc. Therefore, by measuring numerous points and distances between specified locations on the body eg. the distance between two frame mounts, you will be able to keep a constant check on the accuracy of your progress. Finally, you should endeavour to rivet, clamp or bolt additional body parts temporarily to the shell around any repair area so that you can check that panels fit against one another or that clearances are correct eg. fit the doors when replacing the sills. This will show you whether the sills are locating properly and are not interfering with the doors.

This month we will be replacing panels numbered one to three as illustrated plus the stiffener that locates from the rearward edge of number one (the axle top cover) to the boot floor.

For our purposes, because the car is jigged and due to the thoroughness of the restoration, although the chassis legs could have been repaired, we decided that it would be more convenient and would demonstrate the procedure if they were replaced. We don't, however, suggest that this is attempted without a jig as the positioning of the legs is critical for future fitment of the axle.

Although serious rusting is not all that common on the chassis legs, if your car is not jigged, and does require attention, I will explain the method of repair. The protruding bracket on the outer edge of the chassis leg is where water and mud etc. becomes trapped. It is at this point that rusting is likely to occur and, although this may not be too apparent from the outside, the metal inside might have swollen, rusted and be weakened. Internal inspection is therefore necessary and you can do this by cutting out this bracket, allowing you to see whether or not the rusting has progressed across the leg, treating it accordingly if it has, and then replacing the bracket with a new one. If you suspect that no work is going to be required in this area, this could be confirmed if, for some reason, you were to replace the axle top cover, as this would reveal the internals of the chassis leg.

To start the work, we turned our attention to the chassis legs and the rear floor upright (No.2). All the spot welds were drilled out

36 *Removing the rear bulkhead section. Spo welds should always be drilled out accu rately*

underneath and above. If you're not replac ing the chassis legs but the outer ends of th rear floor upright are badly rusted, these sec tions can be bought separately. The nev chassis legs had their black protectio removed with thinners where joins and weld were to be made and the inside was liberall coated with red oxide. The new parts wer then clamped in position.

Our axle top cover had previously been cu open for someone to gain access to the hand

35 *All the spot welds must be carefully dril led out before the chassis legs can be removed.*

37 *The axle top cover rarely rusts except at it outer edges above the chassis member where only local repairs need be made.*

PRACTICAL CLASSICS RESTORATION PROJECT

with the top of the chassis leg. With the section cut down to the right size, it should be fitted in the hole and tacked on, using a hammer if necessary to make it a flush fit. Finish with a continuous weld around the repair which can later be ground down to give a smooth finish.

An alternative method of repair is to use a lap weld. Using a joddler, the metal should be stepped where it will fit around the circumference of the repair. It can then be put in place, making the inside edge smooth, with the overlap in the wheelarch where not only will it not be seen but will also be covered with some sort of protective coating.

As with anything else, these repairs should be cut and welded back one at a time. This will help in limiting the possibility that the body will lose its rigidity and either move or drop down.

Sills

We can now progress to tackle the sills which are both to be replaced and were therefore removed together as described with the photo sequence. It's worth noting that while it may only take a matter of minutes to weld a panel into place, you shouldn't be surprised if it takes somewhere in the order of a couple

38 *The rear bulkhead and chassis legs are now clamped in position ready for welding.*

39 *Welding the chassis legs into place. Note the preparation on the axle top cover where the rust has been cut out.*

brake mechanism and thus needed replacing. We enlarged this hole to give a better access for re-locating our chassis legs. The top cover was then replaced. The boot floor upright stiffener was then located on to the rearward

41 *The new panel has now been welded into place. The old stiffener has been cut out and the new one will fit into the gap between the axle top cover and the boot floor. The section where the inner wing meets the axle top cover has been repaired; another repair section lies beside the file and is about to be fitted into the gap in the wing.*

edge of the axle top cover and was welded in place.

With these panels in place, we concentrated on repairing the inner wing. When rusting is apparent, or where the bodywork metal is evidently thin, the rust should be cut back to good metal, preferably in straight line sections. The cut should be filed smooth and a repair section cut slightly too large out of 20 gauge bright steel, allowing also in this case for a lip to be formed at the bottom to align

of hours to position it correctly. You should expect and be prepared to spend this sort of time on the panels, especially if you want a good finish. It's also important to be aware that these cars can vary slightly and panels will need to be 'modified' on occasions. Before you start hacking a panel to pieces though, you should be sure that it's the panel that is at fault rather than your attempts to fit it.

With the sills removed and the area cleaned up, we advise that the new inner sill is pop-riveted in place (only two or three are required), then offer up the outer sill and any other relevant sections to check that they are going to fit before you do the welding. If you do encounter problems, for example with the door gap, there's not a lot that can be done to remedy the situation, but at least you will be

40 *These brackets should be chiselled off the old panel to be re-used on the new.*

PRACTICAL CLASSICS RESTORATION PROJECT

'E'type!

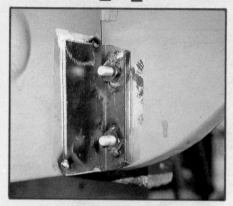

42 *Although the cut at each end should be no more than 1in above the sill to reduce the amount of leading later, we had to go slightly higher due to a fair amount of rust.*

Drill through the spot welds that secure the sills. A little chiselling might also be necessary.

44 *One of the lower frame mounts locates in the sill, the other in the footwell. These should now be welded in.*

47 *Make sure that everything in the inner si is coated in red oxide before the outer sil with its inside face also coated, is welde into position. Note the use of the whi sealant on the edges of the sill.*

able to do a little, thus making the problem less evident.

With the inner sill welded and prepared, the outer sill should be offered up and again riveted in place. Although this was checked even before the inner sill was welded into place, it's wise to double check at this stage especially as the rear stiffener may obstruct the outer sill, forcing it to be dropped by a quarter of an inch or so. If this is the case, this should be rectified now.

The outer sill should locate so that its upper lip is in contact at the rear with the rear bulkhead and the sill can be slid no further rearwards. At the front there should be a distance of no more than 19⅜in between the leading edge of the A post and the end of the sill. If this distance is greater, problems will be encountered when fitting the bonnet. If the rear bulkhead is to have only its two outer sections replaced, the best place to weld these is to the rearward edge of the chassis legs as it

45 *While the rear stiffener tucks up tightly against the rear end, the front stiffener should locate in line with the forward edge of the A post.*

would not be possible to sandwich it withou stripping other parts out. Consequently, th rear section will be about ¹⁄₁₆in further bac than normal. This isn't something tha should concern you and the sill should sti be slid backwards until it contacts with th panel. After all, it's better to have the bonne further back as opposed to being too far for ward, as the latter would result in the forma tion of a gap between the bonnet lip and th bulkhead. Consequently, a strip would hav to be welded to the lip of the bonnet to mak it fit. At least if the sill was too far back, i would mean that only the lip would have t be ground back slightly to prevent interfer ence with the bulkhead, thus making fitting easier and giving a better finish.

43 *With the complete sill assembly removed, the debris should be cleared and tidied up. As the sill was chiselled off, some of it remained and had to be removed by drilling out these spot welds. Note also (because the car is jigged) that for our purposes a section of the floor has also been removed – usually you would separate the sill where it meets the floor.*

46 *Before welding the outer sill, clamp the long front sill stiffener/mounting bracket and the sill end into place.*

Next Month
Frame mounts and a lot more panel work.

PRACTICAL CLASSICS RESTORATION PROJECT
'E' type!

Sponsored by
CONDOR

Part 5

Colin Ford's systematical approach makes the work look easy. But is it? Philip Cooper reports.

PRACTICAL CLASSICS RESTORATION PROJEC

'E' type!

As we left the car in the last issue, Colin Ford (5 South Road, Erith, Kent. Tel: 0322 346584) had just completed the renewal of the sills and the front sill stiffener and the sill end were clamped in position. These should now be welded into place, making sure that the sill end is vertical.

You should be aware that, because the sills need pulling up tightly to fit, this may leave the end slightly rippled. If this happens, the ripples will need to be flattened out, but only do this when the welding has been done otherwise you will risk flattening the curvature of the sill. As can be seen in photograph number 46 in the last issue, there will be a gap between the sill end and the sill. This is correct and will be filled with lead at a later stage. With the sill assembly complete, it's worth checking that the drain hole in the closing panel that locates from the sill to the bulkhead is positioned to ensure efficient drainage.

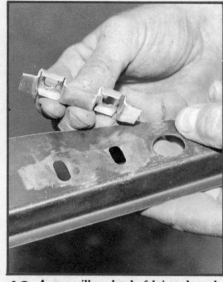

49 *A cage will need to be fabricated to take the captive nuts on this forward facing A post panel. They must not be simply welded in place as they have to be free for adjusting while fitting the bonnet.*

Although we fitted the doors fairly accurately during the work on the sills, it is now necessary to make any fine adjustments to set the doors correctly. The four bolts on the hinge are used to position the doors and, once this has been finalised, the two locating screws should be drilled and secured. If you are re-using a door, it may be wise to weld up the old holes where the previous locating screws were situated before the door is hung in case the new holes have to be drilled in a slightly different place.

With the doors and sills accurately positioned, we progressed to the near side door shut panel, which was rusted and in need of renewal. Where two panels overlap

and are spot welded together, if only one of these panels is to be replaced then a spot weld remover (drill piece) should be used. The spot welds should be either centre punched or shallow drilled with a small drill. The spot weld remover then locates into this initial hole and grinds around the weld, thus allowing the two panels to be separated. An excess of metal will naturally stay on the remaining panel where the welds have been drilled out but this can be simply ground down. Before the panel is welded the locking mechanism should be put on and all the fittings checked with the door in place. The top and bottom of the flange to the inside of the car tucks in behind the panel on to which it locates. Several holes should be punched along the middle section of the flange so that its full length may now be plug welded, as this gives more rigidity than a seam weld here.

One of our bulkhead panels was also deemed to be beyond practical repair and was thus chiselled out. The flanges around this panel were slightly distorted by the chiselling and, therefore, had to be re-flattened before the new panel, supplied by Martin Robey, was offered up and welded into place. So far all of our panels have come from Martin at Poole Road, Camp Hill Industrial Estate, Nuneaton, Warwickshire CV10 9AE (Tel: 0203 386903).

You should now use a paint stripping agent such as Nitromors to remove any remaining paint so that the condition of the metal beneath may be assessed. It was decided earlier in the restoration that the off-side A post panel would be renewed. Heat was therefore applied to the now exposed area of leading that lies above this panel seam. The lead melted back and the seam was revealed. The angle grinder was used to cut along this seam, down the front of the bulkhead and down the rearward face of the post. The inner panel

48 *The flanges on the old panel should be opened up so that the locking mechanism retainer can be transferred to the new panel. Before closing the flanges on the new panel you should make sure that the retainer has a full range of movements.*

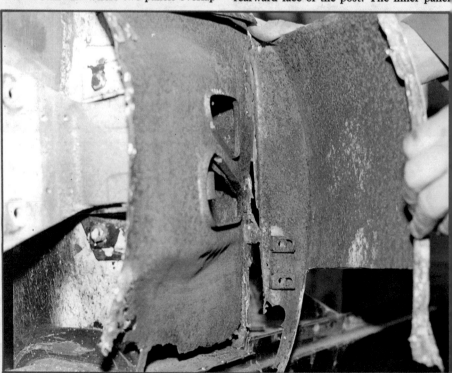

50 *The outer panel was removed to reveal what lay underneath.*

ATION PROJECT

seats are to be replaced, then this is where you should start. Again, the spot weld remover should be used so that the old panel can be removed without damaging the panel that is to remain. With this done, the remaining spot welds around the circumference of the floor pan should be drilled out in the normal manner, remembering to do only one side at a time (advisably the driver's side first), especially if your car is not jigged. If any section of the tunnel is rusted where it meets the floor pan, this should be cut out and mended with repair sections while the floor is still in place to ensure that the repair section mates up to the floor. Because the two sides of the floor pan overlap in the centre of the car underneath the tunnel, you will need to separate them by cutting underneath along

51 *The internal panel was repaired with new sections.*

that we were then faced with, although its appearance might suggest otherwise, was covered with only superficial rusting. This should be treated with an appropriate rust remover such as Ferro-Betol while the more serious rust around the bottom and the edges of the panel should be cut out. With the necessary work completed in this area, the new panels, painted in red oxide, should be welded in place to complete the repair.

The floors are the next on the list for attention and, if the vertical panels behind the

53 *To help in getting the floors in the correct position, it's useful to fit the reaction plate.*

52 *This floor stiffener under the tunnel will need to be drilled out and removed before the floors can be taken out.*

54 *Don't forget to leave an unpainted area on the vertical panel behind the seat where welding is to take place.*

PRACTICAL CLASSICS RESTORATION PROJECT

'E' type!

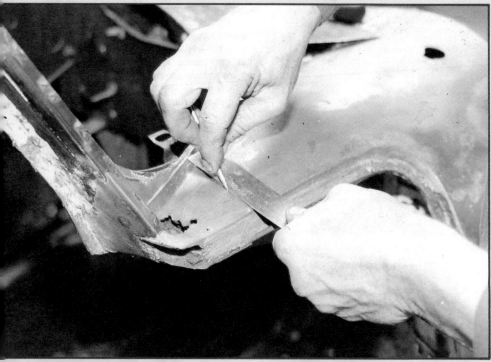

As the vertical panel behind the seat has been removed, the inner area that is now exposed should be treated for any apparent rust. Because it is particularly prone to rust it is wise, if you have an airline, to treat the metal with red oxide, then to blow this with the airline into the seams, thus giving even better protection. When you weld this panel back in you should use a continuous weld where it meets with the inner strengthening bracket on the floor. This will give the added strength that is required by the radius arm mount below the strengthener

To repair the dog's leg, it will be necessary to measure up and make a series of cardboard templates. We started by using a ruler and scribe to draw a line on the dog's leg where the metal would be cut back to – a little way back from the rusting. We then cut some cardboard to the shape of the top repair section that was going to be needed. The metal

55 *Marking up for the repair on the dog's leg.*

56 *The template should be fitted to check that it's correct before the new section is made up*

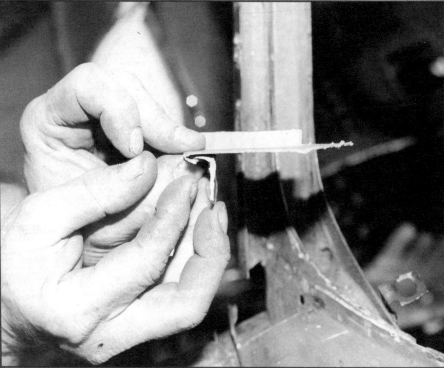

57 *The two repair sections will overlap as shown once they have been cut from their cardboard templates, and formed accordingly.*

the length of the floor pan at about 15in to the passenger side. This will enable the new driver's side floor pan to be fitted without it fouling with the old passenger floor that, at this stage, should still be in place. The old crossmember was cut away where it met the tunnel and, with the new floor in place, the replacement crossmember was fitted for size before it was secured after the floor had been welded in. You mustn't forget here to use thinners to remove the black protective paint from the crossmember and the floor where the crossmember is to be welded.

was then cut back, revealing the extent of the rusting below the top section and again templates were cut to the correct shape and size of the rusted metal that was to be cut out. The last of the bad metal was removed, leaving us with the templates. These were then laid flat on sheets of metal, were scribed around and then cut out. The next stage was to form the necessary lips and flanges to make the new metal fit where the rusted metal was cut out. Finally, we clamped the shapes into place, welded them in and then ground down any excess weld to give a smooth finish. □

| **Next month** |
| The rear end and the roof |

PRACTICAL CLASSICS RESTORATION PROJECT
'E' type!

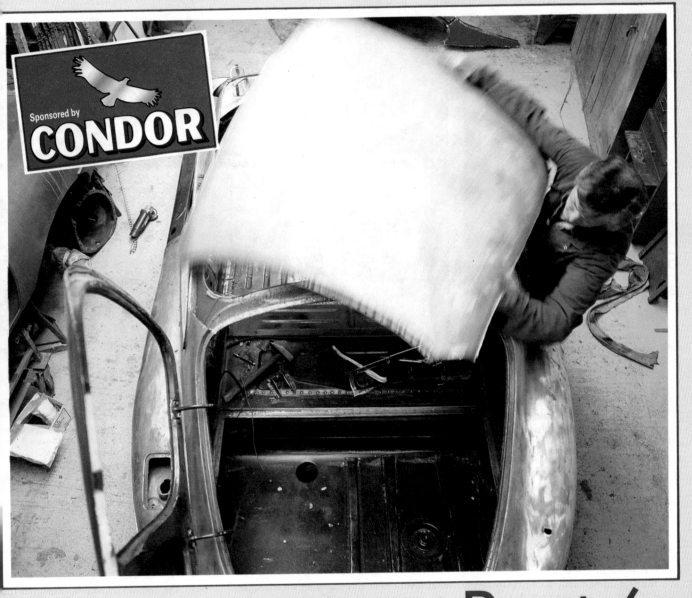

Sponsored by
CONDOR

Part 6

Making a convertible? No chance. Philip Cooper explains what Colin Ford is doing.

'E'type!

59 *Making the repair sections is fairly straightforward but patience and accuracy are essentia*

58 *When producing a repair section for the boot floor stiffener, you must leave an excess of metal which can be folded over to make the return edge. If the repair is small, the return can be bent over in the vice then finished with a dolly once the section is welded on. If the repair is large, this will prove difficult without the correct tools and the return should therefore be formed as a separate piece that can be welded on to the repair section.*

As far as bodywork repairs are concerned, work on the front of the car has now been concluded. Naturally, though, not every car will have rust similar to ours and some of you may find areas around the front that still need treatment. This should be done now using one of the methods previously described.

We can now concentrate on finishing off the rear of the car. The rear boot floor assembly can be bought as one unit from Robey and so, because our floor was fairly well-rusted, it was decided to use this as a replacement rather than trying to make a number of repair sections. Before we cut the floor out, though, a new tonneau panel had to be measured up for fitting to the body. To do this, the new tonneau panel should be offered up to the body and, even though the old panel is still *in situ*, it will be possible to gauge whereabouts this will fit. You should then scribe the body at a safe margin inside where the new panel will fit and then grind down the line, taking care not to go too deep. Next, you should countersink and then drill out the rivets that are securing the back of the panel which, once done, should peel away. Following this, the boot floor should be separated at the seam where it meets the rear wing and chiselled

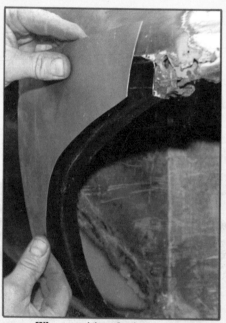

60 *When repairing the inner wing section that runs parallel to its outer half, the correct curvature for the repair section may be formed by moulding it round the outer panel.*

61 *Because of the size of some of these repai sections, it is not possible to bend a return edge. Once a panel is correctly shaped therefore, it should be placed at 90 degree to another sheet of metal. Trace round th curve and cut the flange section out whic can then be welded at the correct angle t the repair section.*

away from the rear of the inner wheelarches. Any remaining spot welds should be drilled out, thus allowing this complete floor assembly to be dropped out. Before moving on, the fuel tank bracket that is welded to the old boot floor should be carefully cut out and saved.

It's likely that the boot floor stiffener in your car will require attention as ours did. If there is rust that needs to be cut out, but is not so severe as to have eaten back the edges, then a template of the stiffener shape should be made before the bad metal is cut out. This will make the process of fabricating a repair section a lot easier. If the rust is more serious, it's as well to buy a new part rather than trying to guess at the shape that it should have

been. With the repair complete, the boo floor assembly should be offered up to check that everything is in order.

With the boot floor assembly removed the lower sections of the rear inner wheelarches are much more easily accessible. Again, as with the boot floor stiffener, cardboard templates should be made up on the rusty panels. Cut the rust back and make repair sections to fit. With the repair section complete, it should be secured with a couple of rivets and the boot floor assembly should again be offered up to check that everything fits.

It should be said that, when panels or repair sections are to be fitted to the body, it's worth offering them up, analysing them and then removing them for any small adjustments, sometimes up to a dozen times if that's how long it takes to get it right. There is no point in taking short cuts here, as you will obviously only be sacrificing the finished result.

With the repairs to the inner wings etc. in the boot area now complete, we begin to offer and size up the boot floor assembly for its final fitting. The fit should be checked by ensuring that the bodylines meet, rather than just simply lining up the flanges. When you believe that you've got it right, the assembly should be removed and all the surfaces that are to be welded should have the black protective paint removed. When welding the assembly to the body, plug welds should be used where the bodywork is holed from having spot welds fully drilled out. The fitting of

65 *Don't forget to weld the petrol tank mounts into the new boot floor assembly.*

62 *The base of the inner rear wheelarches that have now been repaired should be lined with a sealer just before the boot floor assembly is finally fitted.*

63 *With the tonneau closing panel roughly fitted, a plate of 20 gauge metal, 4in long and 2in deep, should be welded with its centre located 4.5in in from the nearside end of the closing panel. This will later have self-tappers screwed into it to secure the rear door stay.*

the back door should also be checked before everything is welded up.

The new tonneau panel can now be fitted by offering it up several times and gradually cutting it to size. The edges of the bodywork on to which the panel will be welded should have a joddled edge so that the panel can be fitted easily with the end result being a better finish. When you have established a good fit, the panel should be removed and the finishing panel that locates underneath the tonneau panel should be put into place, with the tonneau panel placed over the top of it. The finishing panel can then be moved about until it fits correctly, at which stage it should be screwed or riveted into place. Remove the tonneau panel and line up the internal tonneau closing panel. When everything offers up and lines up (including the rear door), weld the panels into place, starting with the finishing panel. Again remember to remove any paint where welds are to be made and coat the rest of the area in red oxide which, if possible, should be blown into the seams.

We then moved on to deal with the rear inner and outer wings. As is usually the case, these were rusted only along their edges and so repair sections will suffice. An outer wing repair section from Robey was offered up against the wing. Colin traced around this, removed the section and drew another line about 2cm inside the first. Using the inside line as a safe margin to work from, Colin then

ground off the rusted section of the wing. The rough cut edge was then filed smooth, so that he wouldn't sustain any injuries while working on the inner wing.

A cardboard template was made of the outer wing repair section, this section then being fitted fairly accurately and screwed into place. It is welded once the inner wing repairs are done, as follows. With the template correctly shaped, it was laid on to a second outer wing repair section, drawn round and cut out. This now became the repair section for the inner wing and was offered up several times and formed and adjusted until it fitted. The new section was joddled to allow for a lap weld. The panels were then tack welded on the outside to help prevent distortion from the heat that builds up during a continuous weld. Another way of helping to reduce heat build-up is to use a heat soak putty. Once done, the weld can be

66 *The leading edge of the wing should be ground away so that the repair section flanges can locate to give an accurate fit when sizing up.*

64 *The rear assemblies that Robey supply are designed for the drophead. The flange shown will need triangles cut out of it so that, with the aid of a dolly, it can be bent over to 90 degrees. The assembly is now correct and the bent flange will help to retain the tonneau closing panel.*

PRACTICAL CLASSICS RESTORATION PROJECT

'E'type!

67 *Use metal cutters when removing the rusted inner wing as this allows you a better feel of the condition of the metal you're cutting. If possible, cut around the location of the bumper flange. After doing this, clean-up the panels.*

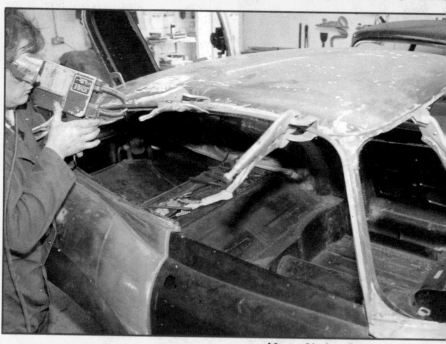

68 *Lay the cardboard template inside the arch and draw around it for the correct angle. Take the template out and cut it to shape.*

ground smooth to disguise the repair and, as the underside of the wheelarches are to be rustproofed, the join will be even less vulnerable to 'weathering'. Clean up the area and paint with red oxide.

We joddled the edge of the outer repair section. As distortion would be very apparent

69 *Drill down through the panel, and leave a length of 3/8in to 1/4in below for the drip. The pipe should be brazed or silver soldered to secure it, making sure that any excess is smoothed off.*

on an external panel, the metal was spot welded at regular intervals. Working backwards and forwards along the edge more welds were added until we effectively had a continuous weld here too. Don't forget to weld the inner and outer panel together where they meet along their edges. Weld the outer repair section where it meets the sill and then grind all welds down until they're smooth.

Some welds on the 'E' type (such as those on the wheelarches) can be found, as original, either continuous or interval spot. If you're going to be leading the car, it's very much up to you what you choose to do. If you're using fillers over the welded areas, however, you should use a continuous weld which should stop damp or even rust prevention liquids from seeping through and ruining the finish.

The final touch to complete the rear end of the car is to fit a drain pipe through the tonneau panel. Originally, 5/16in steel was used but you can use larger if you wish. A smaller bore, however, is liable to block. Obviously you shouldn't use ferrous metal pipe as this will rust. Copper is ideal.

70 *For a smooth finish, joddle the edge where the roof has been cut off across the rear struts. Make sure you de-rust the channels.*

71 *After achieving the correct fit, Colin was very careful to make sure that the new roof panel was fully clamped down before he started welding.*

We have now come to what is probably the most exciting and adventurous stage of this restoration to date. The car as we received it had suffered some damage and when Colin pulled the vinyl off it could be seen that the roof had also been dented. There was only about one square foot that wasn't dented or rippled so to beat out the damage wasn't really a practical proposition. Besides, being at about eye level, the slightest ripple would be detectable even to an untrained eye. The alternative we opted for was to replace the roof.

A complete secondhand roof came from Lynx Cars Ltd, 68 Castleham Road, St Leonards-on-Sea, Sussex TN38 9NU. As our roof struts weren't damaged, Colin decided that it would be best to swap the actual roof panel only.

Using a spot weld remover, and starting at the front, he drilled out the spot welds from the middle, working outwards to help prevent any distortion. It may be necessary to use a chisel and hammer to ease the panels apart, and this too should be done from the middle outwards. The welds down the side were very close and it would have been messy to try to drill these out. Colin therefore used the grinder here. It was necessary to cut across the two rear struts, too. The spot welds can be drilled out at the back and, with the roof removed, weld surfaces were ground smooth. Several captive nuts will also be revealed now and it's worth checking their condition and tapping them out to reduce the likelihood of problems later.

Next month
Fitting the frames & bonnet.

E-TYPE BONNET REPAIR

E-type bonnets needn't always be thrown away. John Williams finds out how you can save them at home without a jig.
Part 1: Dismantling and rebuilding.

The bonnet of the E-type Jaguar consists of a number of panels, most of which are joined by rows of nuts and bolts and screws. There is very little welding in the entire assembly. However, several important flanges are bonded to the bonnet's centre section and to the wings and, on many cars — perhaps a majority — these joints will have broken by now, undermining the rigidity of the bonnet. I wonder how many owners realise that it is not all that difficult to repair these joints and that the whole bonnet can be rebuilt successfully without a jig or other specialised equipment.

To find out what is involved I visited Colin Ford at CF Autos in Erith, Kent (Tel: 0322 346584). Colin is an E-type restoration specialist and has rebuilt more E-type bonnets than he cares to remember. During my visit he was working on the bonnet of a Series 2, 2+2 Automatic but the guidance which I offer here can be applied to all E-type bonnets.

Panels and problems

It will be a lucky owner who has nothing more to do than to dismantle the bonnet which is on the car, reinstate the bonded joints and reassemble the whole thing. In these circumstances the great advantage is that the bonnet is known to have fitted the car and there should be no great problem about making it fit again. Quite a few bonnets which are due for some repairs will need a new under panel, the panel which forms the lower half of the nose of the bonnet. Under panels are available and, apart from the fiddly task of ensuring satisfactory alignment with the centre panel and wings (which certainly will call for some lead loading as I will mention later), fitting them is not difficult and should be well within the scope of the DIY owner.

Replacement outer wing panels are available too and fitting these should present no serious problems as long as their lower rear edges (which, on the finished car, run from the rear of the wheel arches to the bulkhead) are of the correct length. This particular dimension is vitally important if you are buying secondhand wings or ones of doubtful origin, and should be 19.25in to 19.375in. More about this later.

I understand that replacement centre panels are not yet obtainable though a few originals are thought to exist still. The left- and right-hand valances, which incorporate the air scoops and form the inner wings, are not available either. Therefore an owner with a badly rusted or accident damaged bonnet may well be tempted to look around for a secondhand replacement. Colin advises owners to beware of secondhand bonnets. Such a bonnet, which will not be cheap, may or may not be adaptable to fit your car and if it is too short you will have particular difficulties unless you are a very skilled welder.

When shopping for replacement panels bear in mind that parts are not necessarily interchangeable between different E-type models.

Dismantling

Usually the first job is to get the bonnet off

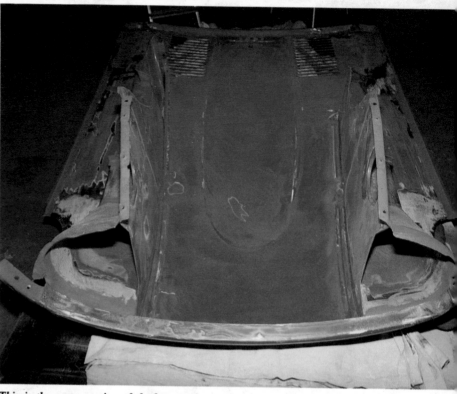

This is the centre section of the bonnet (front towards the camera), upside down and well supported underneath, with the right and left valances standing loosely in position. The pictures are a little ahead of the story in that Colin Ford had bonded both valance flanges before I was summoned to the scene but he then retraced each stage of the job for the camera.

the car. This is fairly straightforward and there is no point in marking anything to provide reference points for use during reassembly. Some of the bonnet's contours and dimensions will change as it is rebuilt and these can be adjusted, once it is back on the car, to produce a good fit.

Colin recommends the liberal use of penetrating oil on all nuts and bolts and screws and suggests that this should be done some days before dismantling is due to start. The hinge bolts and bushes, which attach the hinges to the crossmember on the front frame assembly, are likely to prove stubborn and some heat may be needed to persuade them to loosen, especially if they have not been removed for years. An impact screwdriver may prove useful for starting some of the self-tapping screws which do tend to rust and, for those which do not respond to this treatment, a good set of Mole grips with decent jaws will "crack" the screw so that an ordinary screwdriver will be able to finish the job.

Dismantle the headlamp assemblies, front bumpers etc. and remove the headlamp cowls before removing the bonnet from the car. You will need to provide some form of support for the bonnet so that, when hinged

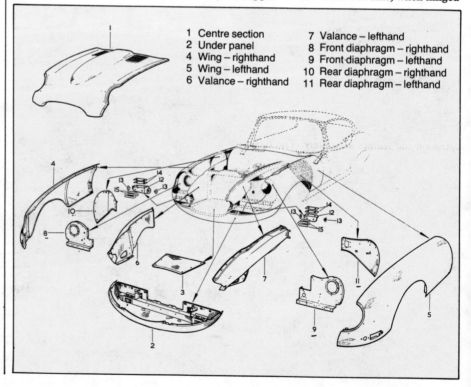

1 Centre section
2 Under panel
4 Wing – righthand
5 Wing – lefthand
6 Valance – righthand
7 Valance – lefthand
8 Front diaphragm – righthand
9 Front diaphragm – lefthand
10 Rear diaphragm – righthand
11 Rear diaphragm – lefthand

E-TYPE

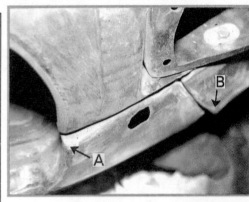

BONNET

forward into a vertical position, it can be supported on its nose at hinge height. Take some care about this arrangement as it will make the first stage of refitting the bonnet to the car so much easier.

Once off the car the bonnet can be turned upside down and supported evenly throughout its entire length and width. It is important to support the centre section adequately because, despite its compound curves, it will distort quite readily once other panels have been disconnected. Furthermore, if it proves necessary to make new flanges for the right- and left-hand valances they will have to be matched to the fore and aft curvature of the centre section.

Once the bonnet is off the car and supported you can start dismantling the front diaphragms and the under panel, then the rear diaphragms and wings and finally the right and left valances. You will finish up with a lot of assorted nuts and bolts, screws, self-tapping screws etc. and numerous washers. It would be worthwhile to use a number of small labelled containers for these items so that the correct screws etc. come readily to hand when reassembling.

Now is the time to give everything a thorough clean and inspection, removing rust down to bare metal as you do so. Sort out which items can be repaired and which of them will have to be replaced. By this stage you will have noticed that the front and rear diaphragms and the right and left valances are attached to flanges which, in turn, are attached to the centre section of the bonnet and/or the wings by a bonding material rather than by welds. These flanges are not available and will have to be made if the originals have deteriorated to the extent that they cannot be repaired. You may well find that where these flanges have broken away there will be rust on the centre section or wings. Having cleaned back to bare metal and repaired as necessary do not paint the areas to which the flanges will be bonded.

Preparation for reassembly

If any flanges on your bonnet have broken free you will need to clean off the old bonding material (and any rust which has developed) and, in doing so, you will destroy any marks on the panels which would enable you to reposition the flanges accurately. The most critical part of the whole operation is repositioning the flanges which attach the right and left valances to the centre section of the bonnet. Yet you don't need to mark the panel and neither do you need some form of jig, though a jig could save time if you are doing a lot of this type of work.

To find the correct positions for the flanges which have broken loose all you have to do is reassemble the main components of the bonnet. With the centre section of the bonnet upside down, and supported exactly as it was when it first came off the car, the right and left valances can be placed in their approximate positions (where they will stand without support) while the under panel is laid across them to indicate how far apart they should be at their forward ends. The under panel can be

With the under panel laid across the forward ends of the valances and bolted up loosely the wings can be fitted.

When refitting the wings don't forget the spacing washers which separate the wings from the centre section.

Next it is the turn of the diaphragm panels (mudguards). The rear diaphragms (nearside shown here) will confirm the position of the rear ends of the valances.

The front diaphragms bolt to the wings, valances and under panel.

Now is the time to look for and rectify significant misalignments between adjacent panels at the front of the bonnet. Here (arrow A) the new under panel not only curves too sharply around the air intake aperture but its edge has too small a radius to match the centre section in the same area. It doesn't match the wing (arrow B) either. These faults can be reduced by moving the panels as described in the text and lead loading will take care of the final finish.

Where too much metal cannot be adjusted to fit you may have to grind off the excess but don't do this until you are sure that it is the only solution to the problem.

REPAIR

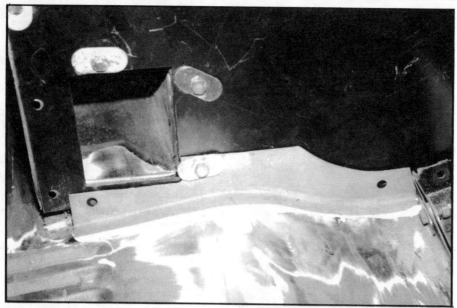

The short flanges which attach the diaphragms to the centre section can be bonded into place during the second assembly stage. The correct positions for these flanges will be obvious once the diaphragms are bolted in position.

bolted into position and you may have to "adjust" one or two bolt holes to match those in adjacent panels if you are working with a replacement underpanel. Next, fit the rear diaphragms which span the gaps between the rear ends of the valances and the outer wings — thus locating the rear ends of the valances — followed by the front diaphragms and the wings. Finally drop the square grille into its position between the valances to confirm the correct gap between them.

By this stage the main parts of the bonnet will be together again though you needn't use *all* the nuts and bolts and screws for this trial assembly. Check the external surfaces of the outer panels, and particularly the underpanel, centre section and wings to see that they are reasonably well aligned. Any major discrepancies should be put right at this stage. Check the position of the underpanel in relation to the wheel arches and adjust it if necessary — you may need to unroll the underpanel and re-roll it in the appropriate way to lengthen or shorten it. Mind you, if you are working with all the same panels which came

Take each flange in turn, apply some Sikaflex and locate the flange with a couple of screws. Its diaphragm is already bolted in position at this stage and it is worth adding more bonding material when the flange is in place. Tighten the screws and leave to cure.

off the car there shouldn't be any real problems.

The adjustment of these panels will entail slackening bolts, moving the panels in relation to each other, clamping them in the new position with Mole grips and/or welding clamps and tightening the bolts again. Lead loading is required where centre section front flange and forward flange of wing meet on all post-Series I cars and this is best done when the bonnet is back on the car and all the adjustments have been completed.

If all is well at this stage you can take it that all the panels which should be joined together by bonded flanges are correctly positioned

too, and the next step is to bond the right a left valance flanges into place.

Bonding the flanges

If you have done your cleaning adequatel bonding the flanges into place couldn't more simple. Colin uses Sikaflex 2 Automotive, which is described as "a o component adhesive and sealing material permanent elasticity on a polyurethane ba with accelerated setting power". It comes a 310cc cartridge from Sika Ltd, Welw Garden City, Herts. It is applied by using cartridge gun of the sort used with domes sealants but it is a tremendously strong adh sive and should not be confused with any the domestic sealants which are available similar packings. There are other bondi products but Colin finds Sikaflex 2 Automotive very reliable in that it will s fully overnight.

It is only the valance flanges which shou be bonded at this stage. Apply plenty Sikaflex to the underside of each flang Then position each flange carefully, pressi it into place on the centre panel and in conta with its valance and ensuring that the bo holes line up correctly. Fit two or three bol to hold it in place. Having fitted these tw flanges you should leave the whole assemb undisturbed overnight while the bond sets.

Colin dismantles the bonnet the day aft bonding these flanges so that he can chec that the bonding material has cured all t way through. Surplus Sikaflex can be trin med away at this stage and the flanges an surrounding area can be painted as nece sary. Then the reassembly work starts a over again and, while this is in progress, th short flanges for the front and rear diaph ragms are positioned and bonded.

There is reinforcement under the rear edg of the bonnet's centre panel which is partl spotwelded and partly bonded (about nin inches from each side) to the panel. If th needs re-bonding it should be done after a the necessary adjustments have been finishe with the bonnet on the car.

NEXT MONTH:
Fitting and re-aligning the bonnet.

E-TYPE BONNET REPAIR

Part 2: Refitting the bonnet and adjustments on the car.

L ast month I suggested that dismantling and rebuilding the bonnet of a Jaguar E-type is within the scope of a DIY enthusiast and the story ended with the bonnet reassembled and ready to go back on the car. The next job is to attach the bonnet to the car and adjust it to fit.

Alignment on the car

First of all make sure that you have plenty of shims which fit behind the hinges and make more if necessary, using the originals as patterns. Note that there are two types of shims and it certainly helps to have both types. Refit the hinges to the bonnet away from the car and use as many shims as you can. If anything, the bonnet should be too high at the front and too far forward when first refitted to the car. This should ensure that it will not collide with other parts of the car and cause damage. It is helpful to have an assistant at this stage to help you lower the bonnet a little at a time while watching both sides to see that the valances don't strike the radiator or other parts and that the rear edges of the wings do not collide with the front of the bulkhead or with its outer edges. Check at this stage that the rear end of each wheelarch (where it joins the horizontal lower edge of the wing) does not rest on the sill on each side. If it does, it means that the bonnet is too low at the front and needs more shims above the hinges to raise it.

Now you can set about adjusting the alignment of the bonnet as a whole. Carry out one adjustment at a time and then check all around the bonnet to see what effect it has had before making another adjustment. Bear in mind that if one side of the bonnet looks correct it does not necessarily follow that the other side will be correct, too, and that many of the adjustments which you may carry out will have some effect on *both* sides of the bonnet whether you want them to or not.

Start by ensuring that the bonnet is positioned centrally in relation to the rest of the car. This is done by sighting along the tops of the wings and eliminating any discrepancies by moving the bonnet sideways after slackening the hinge bolts.

Next, make sure that you have a parallel gap of the correct width between the rear edge of the centre section and the bulkhead. This is adjustable by the shims which are in front of (rather than those on top of) the hinges. Start by getting a parallel gap by adding shims to the hinge which is on the same side as the narrow end of the gap (or subtracting them from the other side) and then increase or decrease the width of the gap by adding or subtracting an equal number of shims on both sides.

Now for a slightly more complicated manoeuvre! You will want parallel gaps of the correct width down the vertical rear edges of the wings and along the lower horizontal edges. You will also want the rear corner of the wheelarch on each side to coincide exactly with the corner of the sill. This is the vital datum point and it is where you are most likely to come unstuck with a secondhand bonnet, especially if it is too short. The adjustment of these gaps could involve both sets of shims on both hinges. The shims above the hinges should enable you to make

If, when removing the bonnet from the car, you took some trouble to arrange a platform to support the bonnet in its vertical position at hinge height, you will find it much easier to refit the bonnet to the car.

Clean up the ends of the horizontal rail at the front of the front subframe which supports the bonnet and make sure that the bushes and bolts will fit easily before putting the bonnet in position. If any part of the car's front frame assembly has been damaged or distorted this will have to be put right before fitting the bonnet.

Each bonnet hinge assembly consists of a casting, a metal bush which passes through the casting and some way into the subframe crossmember, and a couple of nylon bushes which surround the metal bush in the casting.

Four bolts attach the hinge casting to the bonnet (this is the offside hinge — the outer edge of the bonnet is to the right) and there are two types of shims. Shims with a single long slot should be inserted in front of the hinge from the centre of the bonnet and the other type, which has two slots, goes on top of the hinge.

The first step after refitting the bonnet to the car is to lower it slowly, checking that the valances do not collide with the radiator or with anything else in the engine compartment and that the bonnet will sit right down on the edge of the bulkhead without striking the front or sides of the bulkhead with the lower corners of the wings. Here the bonnet is too far back on the car and needs more shims in front of the hinges.

When this bonnet sits down on the bulkhead it will be necessary to widen the gap across its upper edge on the offside by adding an extra shim or two in front of the offside hinge. Don't assume that as each adjustment is done it is finished with — for example, having got the gaps right you may find that you need to re-centralise the bonnet again.

the gaps parallel and to achieve the correct width for the horizontal gap. You may add or subtract shims in front of the hinges to achieve the correct width for the vertical gap and this will adjust the bulkhead to centre the panel gap at the same time while aligning the corners of the panels at the datum points to which I have referred already.

If you have a satisfactory bonnet you probably will not need to worry about specific measurements. However, the length of the lower rear edges of the wings should be equal at 19.25in to 19.375in. If the wings are too long in this respect they can be shortened — if they are too short you have got problems. Adding metal to wings and centre section requires a high degree of welding skill.

The removal of metal, using a grinder, should be regarded as a last resort. It requires

E-TYPE BONNET REPAIR

The forward corner of the sill (arrowed) should coincide with the rear corner of the wheelarch on the wing on each side of the car. These are the datum points and, although the wings can be shortened or (with difficulty) lengthened, it would be well worth measuring both the sills and the wings (especially if the wings are replacements) to see whether any problems can be anticipated. This would be especially worthwhile if you are dealing with a car whose sills may have been inexpertly repaired at some time.

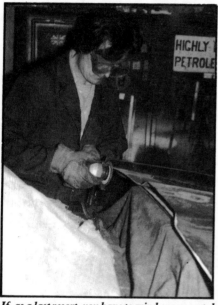

If, as a last resort, you have to grind excess metal off the wings and centre section, be sure to use gloves and goggles and cover the windscreen — the debris from a grinder can easily ruin a windscreen.

immense care but is within the scope of the average DIY enthusiast. If the wings are too long (so that they would overlap the bulkhead when aligned with the front ends of the sills or are just a shade too long to allow gaps of the correct width) mark their edges very carefully and grind away the excess metal a little at a time — better to remove too little than too much.

Other adjustments to the rear edges of the bonnet centre section and wings should be left until after you are satisfied with the overall alignment of the bonnet. Obtaining the correct curve at the rear edges of the wings depends on having some room for manoeuvre in the bolt holes where the rear diaphragms are attached and at the bracing brackets under the upper rear edges of the wings. If you are working on the same panels that came off the car you should have little trouble at this stage but, if you have changed the wings, you may or may not have to make substantial adjustments now. Elongate some bolt holes if

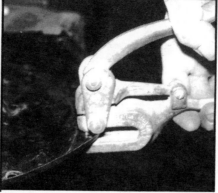

When it comes to adjusting the holes in the rear diaphragm (mudguard) panels this type of punch would be a useful tool to borrow. A cone shaped rasp for use in the electric drill would be useful where you cannoy gain access to a panel with the punch.

necessary so that, having slackened the bolts, you can alter the curvature of the wing panel before tightening the bolts again and checking how much improvement you have achieved. It has been suggested that the characteristic lozenge-shaped washers found on the E-type and other Jaguars are not that shape (and thickness) without reason this being that they are equally suitable for covering round or elongated bolt holes.

Re-bonding the bracing rail to the rear edge of the centre bonnet section should be left until you are satisfied that the edge sits down nicely along the edge of the bulkhead, neither too low and therefore tending to lift the wings, nor too high and leaving gaps.

Lead loading

The following notes concerning lead loading may prove helpful to beginners though they are not intended to constitute a detailed guide.

If you have not tried this before let me assure you that it is not as difficult a job as you may think. Mind you, you will need a little practice to get good results and, at first anyway, you will probably apply too much lead, leaving a lot of filing to be done in your efforts to achieve the correct contours.

Start by cleaning, very thoroughly, the area around the joints to be leaded. When

Jaguar E-Type Parts Prices

The following prices, inclusive of VAT, are based on those shown in the latest stock list from Martin Robey Sales Ltd, Pool Road, Camp Hill Industrial Estate, Nuneaton, Warwickshire CV10 9A1. Tel: 0203 386903. A range of prices against an item indicates that prices vary depending on the model.

Under panel	£200.10-£238.05
Wing	£181.13
Front diaphragm	£23.58-£27.32
Rear diaphragm	£10.35
Bonnet support frame	£108.10
Picture frame (supports stoneguard)	£101.20-£120.75
Main side frame (right or left)	£271.69-£287.50
Air duct lower panel	£4.32
Complete bonnet – Series 1/2/3	£1201.75
Complete bonnet – Series 1½	£1527.78

this has been done properly you should see bare metal with no blemishes or spotty remnants of deep rust. A rotating wire brush on an electric drill is ideal for this job.

Colin uses Starchem solder paint. This comes in a plastic pot. Other brands are available in tins but if you don't use them very often it can be difficult to get their lids off. The solder paint is brushed on to the area to be leaded and is then heated just enough to make it become shiny. Remember that too much heat will distort the panels — the last thing you need! When the paint has become shiny you wipe if off with a damp cloth, looking for any areas in which it is not uniformly shiny. If you find such areas then your initial cleaning wasn't thorough enough, the lead probably won't stick and you will have to start at the beginning again.

Next, heat the lead and apply it firmly to the panel, spreading it with a wooden spatula. If there is too much heat at this stage the lead will simply flow off the job on to the floor. Keep clear of any places where the lead

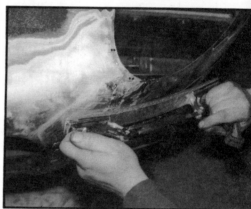

If anything, you should err on the side of putting on too much lead — you can remove the excess later with an adjustable file as shown here.

will flow or drip should you inadvertently overheat it, otherwise it will go straight through your overalls and make holes in your anatomy. On the other hand you need to keep it soft enough to be workable with the spatula so that you can shape it to something like the desired end result. If you are not experienced enough to achieve an ideal result it is probably better to apply too much lead and rely on removing the excess later with an adjustable file.

And finally . . .

At the end of the job you may have used fewer shims, or more shims, even using the same bonnet. It has been dismantled and rebuilt and there are so many bolts and screws that the cumulative effect of a few slight differences in the relative positions of panels may well give rise to a different number of shims being needed. On the other hand it may well be that the bonnet didn't fit particularly well previously and, having followed this article, you have improved it considerably!

You may be lucky enough to complete the alignment work in a few hours or it may take a couple of days. Either way a good result will be its own reward and particularly as the bonnet contributes so much to the spectacular lines of the E-type Jaguar. □

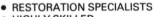

PRACTICAL CLASSICS RESTORATION PROJECT
'E' type!

Sponsored by CONDOR

Part 7

Philip Cooper translates Colin Ford's actions into print as the final bodywork repairs are completed.

PRACTICAL CLASSICS RESTORATION PROJEC

'E' type!

All the panel and body repairs on your 'E' type should now be complete. Because there are various weld seams etc. left over from the work on the body, the next stage will be to smooth these out and prepare the car for spraying.

Although it's possible to use fillers to smooth the seams over, Colin (C.F. Autos, 5 South Road, Erith, Kent. Tel: 0322 346584) favours the use of lead. If you choose this method you will, of course, need a good blow torch, plenty of lead sticks, a dreadnought file and a suitable applicator.

After grinding the weld surface smooth, Colin tinned the area and then applied heat until the surface took on a tarnished appearance. Using a moist cloth, the surface was wiped, giving the area a very shiny finish. With the lead stick held in a pair of grips close to the body, it was warmed, as was the metal, with a flame that was not too vigorous. As the lead became more fluid, Colin dabbed it off on to the body while keeping the flame on the rest of the stick and the body at the same time to maintain an overall temperature.

With the lead on the body, Colin heated it to keep it in a molten state so that it was workable and used a maplewood paddle to pat it out evenly across the surface. The paddle had to be tallowed first, though, to prevent the lead from sticking to it and to help maintain the heat. Don't allow the lead to run. With an even set, the lead was allowed to cool slightly before it was filed into the correct and smooth shape.

72 *Last month's roof panel swap – a job that I certainly haven't heard of being attempted before – turned out a treat.*

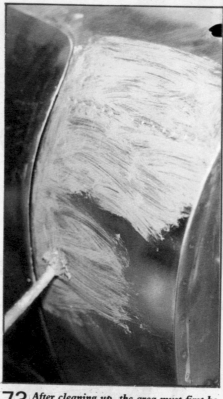

73 *After cleaning up, the area must first be tinned with a solder paste.*

A few points to note. When heating off any old lead you must use goggles as it has the tendency to 'spit'; when heated, air pockets expand and blow outwards. Don't be tempted to use water to cool the lead down as it may go slightly powdery. Don't try to cut corners by grinding lead down. It's dangerous because the disc may clog and build up heat but, more importantly, think about the dust – lead poisoning. Finally, if you find a recess in the lead as you're filing down, the trick is to apply enough heat to allow more lead to take up the space but to ensure that the rest of the surface doesn't melt down.

Leading is also a very useful method of getting the gaps around the doors even. Although the door must be correctly hung first, it doesn't matter too much if the door settles fractionally too high as it's likely that once all the innards have been put in, the door will drop slightly under the weight. It's also wise to fit the door seals to check that the doors fit and to ensure that the seals don't bounce the doors back out.

The bulkhead should now be thoroughly cleaned up and prepared for spraying as should the frames which should have returned from being etch coated. Although it will be very apparent if there is any serious rusting on the outside of the frames, you must remember that rusting may occur inside the frames where it will be more difficult to detect. It's very appropriate therefore that one of the early stages of the coating process is sandblasting. Blasting should show up any weaknesses but it's as well to tap along the length of the frames afterwards to listen for any irregularities that indicate weak metal. Although sandblasting in this application is a good thing, Colin advises very strongly indeed against its use on any body panels whatsoever. He's seen too many bodies rippled and ruined by the process.

The newly painted frames will need to be thoroughly Waxoyled for rust prevention and the frames should be hung up and allowed to dry before they are put back on the car.

With the frames re-instated in the opposite manner to which they were taken off, we are now able to start fitting up the bonnet. Our original bonnet was beyond repair, so a new one came from Lex Mead. If you intend to use your old one and it needs repairing, this

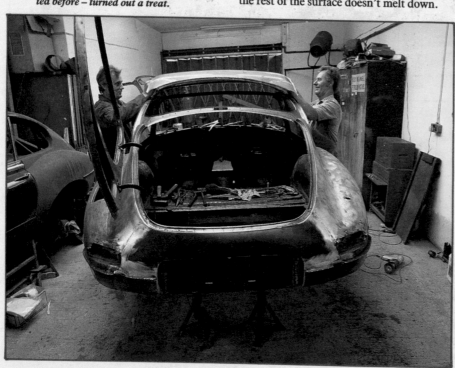

74 *Although it may start to look fairly messy, you shouldn't worry about that at this stage.*

RACTICAL CLASSICS RESTORATION PROJECT

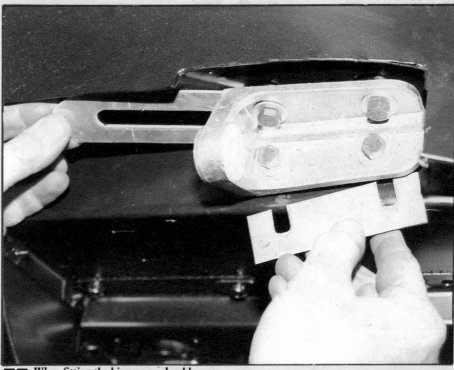

77 *When fitting the hinges you should use as many shims as possible to start with. This way, on the first attempt, the bonnet will be more likely to shut as it will be as far forward and as high as possible. Hopefully therefore, nothing should catch and thus there will be no damage.*

was covered in *Practical Classics* in the July 1988 issue. With the hinges fitted, Colin took a measurement between the two hinge mounts and checked this against the distance between the hinges now secured on the bonnet to ensure that everything was going to fit when the bonnet was offered up. To get the bonnet to fit it was necessary to keep adjusting the number of shims under the hinges and it should be noted that, on a bad one, you may have to add or subtract shims some 20 or more times. It is therefore important that you should not overtighten the hinge bolts after an adjustment, because tightening the bolts

up so many times is likely to damage the threads and leave you in a bit of trouble. As our bonnet seemed to be taking on a somewhat uneven fit, Colin loosened the bolts from a couple of the panels that make up the bonnet. This released some of the rigidity and the bonnet fell into place more evenly. The bolts were then re-tightened. You may have to trim off some of the bonding sealer to give a cleaner appearance under the bonnet.

A good way of checking if the bonnet is well-aligned is by eye. Looking from the back of the car, see how closely the top of the doors line up with the bonnet seams and compare both sides of the car. No matter how concentrated your efforts are, all this may not be sufficient to finish the fit. It is often neces-

78 *When the bonnet is attached, wooden blocks should be placed on the floor for the nose to rest on when the bonnet is opened.*

75 *The dreadnought file can be curved to help you get the right shape.*

76 *The frames should be filled with Waxoyl and then emptied to ensure good protection. The threads must be tapped to clear them before the frames are fitted.*

PRACTICAL CLASSICS RESTORATION PROJECT

'E'type!

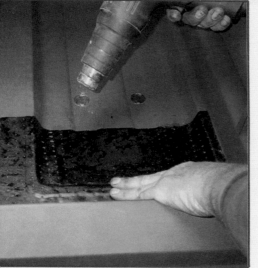

79 *Put the grille in to check that it fits.*

81 *The insides of the rear wheelarches should be painted with red oxide. All seams here and inside the car should then be sealed.*

80 *When sound deadening material is heated it will become more fluid, allowing you to work it into the contours of the floor.*

82 *Sections of cant rail from an XJS can be used on the 'E' type.*

tion. The rest of the floor, inner sills, crossmembers and the rear of the bulkhead etc. were also coated in red oxide.

Colin then turned his attentions to the exterior of the car. This now has to be prepared for painting. The black protective paint on the bonnet and boot assembly does not need to be removed, and it is a good protective base to start from. The rest of the body should be cleaned up (perhaps with an electric wire brush) until you are left with bare shiny metal.

83 *This chrome light surround, as with a lot of our other replacements parts, came from Martin Robey, Pool Road, Camp Hill Industrial Estate, Nuneaton, Warwickshire CV10 9AE, Tel: 0203 386903.*

sary to unfold edges, to grind an edge back or even to add extra length to an edge. If you do have to grind, always be wary of the rough edge that is left. One final point is that you shouldn't use the fitting pins to locate the bonnet. It's far better to obtain a true fit rather than relying on the pins to pull the bonnet in.

It's now time to clean up and paint. With all the repairs on the internal panels and the floors etc. having been finished a long time ago, the inside of the car should be thoroughly cleaned and swept out. Any superficial rust that has set on the bare metal should be removed with a suitable product such as Ferro Betol. With this done, Colin applied generous quantities of red oxide to all the seams and, using an airline, it was blown into and through the seams for extra protec-

Finally, before spraying, fittings such as the bumpers and light surrounds etc. should be put on to the car to check they fit correctly. We did encounter a slight problem in that the screw holes in our light surround were not quite in line with the captive nuts in the bonnet. Colin therefore carefully chiselled off the nuts that weren't aligned, welded up the holes and then ground the weld smooth. The surround was then positioned and temporarily secured while new holes were drilled in the correct place. Colin then welded the nuts into place below the new holes. To finish off, a scribe was used to draw around the inner circumference on the flange below; it was then neatly trimmed. Don't forget to fit the radius arm mounts with steel rivets.

Next Month
Re-building the rear axle.

PRACTICAL CLASSICS RESTORATION PROJECT
'E' type!

Sponsored by
CONDOR

Part 8

Colin Ford strips down the rear axle. Philip Cooper reports.

'E'type!

After concluding last month's work (finishing off the body), Colin Ford prepared the car and then sprayed it in British Racing Green. The technique of spraying has been extensively covered in previous issues of the magazine. We're now faced with an empty shell and so it's time to turn our attention to the mechanics so that they can be re-conditioned and prepared for installation. We're starting with stripping the axle.

Before beginning this job, especially if your axle has been standing for a while, it's advisable to spray the various nuts and bolts with a freeing solution and then leave it to soak for a couple of days.

With the whole axle inverted, Colin began by unbolting the bottom plate. Following this the bolt that secures the shock absorbers through the lower outer fulcrum was undone. The hub has to be supported to prevent it from dropping down when the bolt has been taken out. The two individual bolts at the other end of the shock absorbers are then removed.

The lower outer fulcrum dummy shaft that holds the bearing and shims can be removed at this stage. However, if it's going to be rebuilt anyway, it's not strictly necessary to do this now as the strip down can be completed with it still in place. After the lower inner fulcrum has been released, the fulcrum can be removed – note any washers found here.

Unbolt the drive shaft from the disc and carefully remove and keep the camber adjustment shims, labelled up as per the side from which they came. Remove the handbrake compensator linkage that is on top of the axle casing. Although ours had been welded up by a previous owner, it should have a clevis and split pin assembly. Take off any remaining brake pipes, roll the axle over, and undo the four axle case mounting bolts that hold the differential to the carrier – these should be wired.

With the diff out of the casing, take out the two pivot bolts and remove the handbrake caliper by wriggling it free. If you encounter problems removing some of the bolts, don't wait until something breaks before thinking of an alternative method of removal. If you force it and break it, you will have hours of fun drilling it out.

On the inboard side of the discs there are two large caliper locating bolts that need to be removed. These are both wired. Remove the discs and, once again, keep the shims that centralise the discs in the calipers. Before the differential is turned upside down to remove the inner fulcrum carrier, the breather should be unscrewed to prevent it from being broken.

The spacing tube should now just tap out of the inner fulcrum carrier. Two bolts which need to be undone will now be revealed, thus

84 *These shims will be visible once the bottom plate has been taken off. Ours were all rusted away b* *what was left was kept for reference.*

85 *Before you remove this bolt you will have to support the hub.*

86 *Knock this bolt out to release the hub assembly from the lower outer fulcrum.*

ACTICAL CLASSICS RESTORATION PROJECT

37 *When unbolting the drive shaft it will be necessary to jam the discs with a crow-bar to prevent them from turning.*

38 *It was necessary to apply heat to this pivot bolt to free it.*

llowing the carrier to be removed. Take the shims out. If the heads of any of the nuts or bolts seem a little suspect, then an impact socket may be very handy. If the nut or bolt head is already a little rounded then try fitting a slightly smaller socket. An application of heat will help greatly.

Remove the universal joint dust covers on the drive shafts by unscrewing the Jubilee clips and drilling out the pop rivets. The cover will fall into two halves and may be removed. If you extract the split pin in the hub it will be possible to unscrew the hub retaining bolt. Separate the splined hub in the middle of the hub carrier from the drive shaft. With this done you can drift the splined hub out from the hub carrier. If it won't tap through, get it pressed out by a garage rather than persevering until something gets broken. Tap out the inner bearing and oil seal.

Then tap out the outer race of the inner and outer bearings along with the oil seal. You will need to tap the races quite hard but don't be too heavy handed.

Take out the grease seals from the outer fulcrum using a suitable drift. Then knock out the inner bearings and the spacing tube. There will also be some shims for you to look out for. Finally, knock out the outer bearing race which is notched, using an appropriate drift to gain a good purchase.

Theoretically, you should be able simply to knock out the universal joints on the drive shaft. This is rarely the case, though, and you will probably have to press them out in a vice. Failing this there are plenty of companies

89 *The nut in the centre of the hub will probably require about 100lb pressure to move it. An extension on your ratchet may therefore be needed to give the required leverage.*

90 *You will need a hub puller to separate the splined hub from the drive shaft. These are available through the Jaguar Enthusiasts Club or, alternatively, you could try a local Jaguar dealer.*

91 *Use a suitably sized socket and extension to drift the splined hub from the centre of the hub carrier.*

PRACTICAL CLASSICS RESTORATION PROJECT
'E' type!

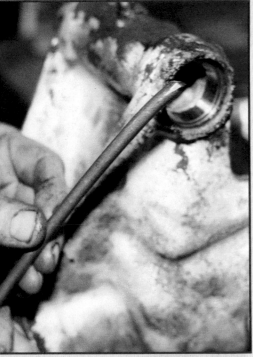

94 *You shouldn't really attempt to dismantle the diff unless you know what its all about.*

92 *A tool such as this is ideal for tapping out the outer bearing race in the outer fulcrum.*

95 *Our diff was in surprisingly good condition (especially these friction plates) but we chose to replace all the bearings nevertheless.*

96 *All the surfaces of every moving part will need to be ruthlessly examined for pitting or signs that the hardening has been worn away.*

93 *Dismantle the handbrake mechanism.*

who are set up to do this for you, returning a correct and balanced unit.

Dismantle the handbrake caliper by taking out the hinge pin and the screw that retains its case. The pawl assembly will then be revealed. Take it out, pull off the internal spring and unbolt the pads. Fix the caliper into a vice and undo the centre nut. Take off the bracket and remove the pads. Unbolt the piston assemblies from the caliper body. Pull

the casing off the piston. If this proves difficult you can attach an air line to the casing and blow the piston out. Use the lowest possible pressure and keep one hand firmly on the casing. Alternatively, try to prise off the casing gently, taking care not to scratch the inner surface.

Repairing the internals of any differential, but particularly a Powr-Lok or limited slip Jaguar diff, is a specialist job. It also requires several tools not to be found in the normal workshop. What we suggest is that it is left in the capable hands of somone who knows what they're doing. We have therefore li-

mited our coverage of this stage because if you're going to tackle it yourself then you'll know what you're doing and what to look for. If you're not experienced with diffs, even if you do strip it down, you probably won't notice the more subtle tell-tale signs of damage and wear that are so obvious to a trained eye. You will therefore end up taking it to a specialist anyway so that it can be examined and fixed if need be.

Next Month
Re-assembly of the rear axle.

PRACTICAL CLASSICS RESTORATION PROJECT

'E'type!

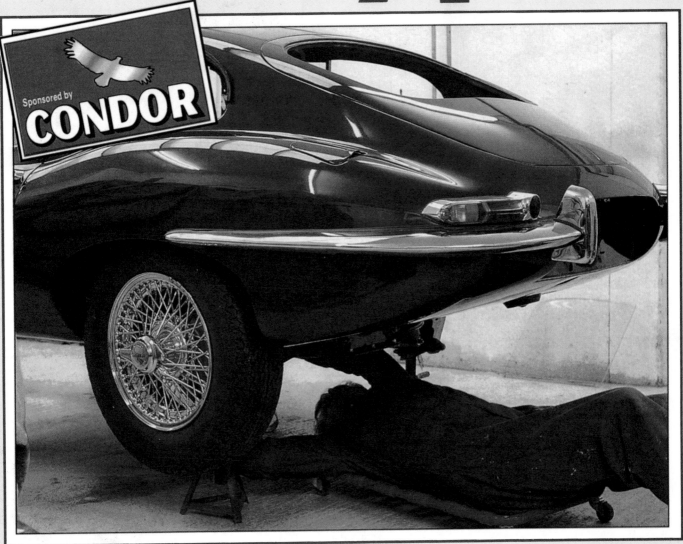

Sponsored by
CONDOR

Part 9

Philip Cooper reports while Colin Ford carries out the exacting process of the rear axle re-build.

PRACTICAL CLASSICS RESTORATION PROJEC

'E' type!

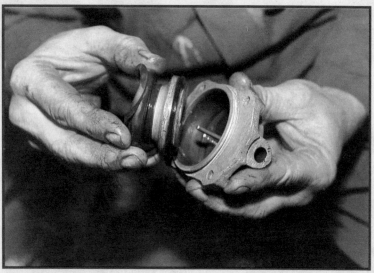

The painting and polishing, (that has been going on in the background), is now all finished and, as I am sure those of you who saw the car at Alexandra Palace will agree, it looks superb. The paints were kindly supplied by Glasurit Paints Tel: 0895 431155. With all the rear axle components restored/repaired as required, Colin Ford (C.F. Autos, 5 South Road, Erith, Kent, Tel: 0322 346584) can now re-build the rear axle.

Sit the differential on some wood so that the brake discs can rotate. Later cage fitment will also be easier with the diff elevated. After reconditioning and cleaning up, the diff housing was painted with Smoothrite so all the threads will need to be tapped through and the paint will need to be removed from the surfaces on to which the calipers locate. The bolts that hold the inner fulcrum mounting bracket, and the diff, to the axle cage have Whitworth threads while all the rest are UNF so make sure you use the correct tap.

Put the discs in place (the correct way around) and, using spacers, pinch up the bolts to hold the disc true. Offer up the calipers using the old shims (if they're good) and, after greasing, fit spring washers to and locate the two correct bolts – those with holes for wiring. The importance of tapping threads is highlighted here as the holes into which these bolts locate must be clear enough to enable the bolts, that are awkwardly placed, to be finger-tightened first. Fitting the calipers can be tricky when you're trying to keep the shims in place and we advise that the top bolt is located first.

You can use galvanised or stainless steel wire (available from boat yards) on the bolts but be careful of the latter as it is hard and spiteful. We put Copper-Slip along the length of the wire and through the holes in the bolt head. We pushed the wire through

97 *After lubricating with silicone fluid fit the rubber seal on to the piston, push the flat washer over the top and fit the cupped seal into place. Press the piston into the cylinder and fit the cupped seal over the outer lip. Bolt the assembly to the caliper.*

99 *Smear the pawl assembly with grease to keep out moisture as much as to lubricate. It must move freely.*

one head, gave it a few turns, and then fed the other end through the other bolt and a few more twists finished the job. The wire should be taut not tight.

The handbrake must now be re-built and, no matter how good the pads look, they should be replaced. They are cheap and a new set correctly adjusted should last for years. Grease up the inside and the outside of the trunnion block (to prevent moisture from seeping in) and make sure that it moves freely otherwise it may cause damage, and it certainly won't adjust. The self-adjuster should also be greased (especially the threads) as these often seize up and are thus a common MoT failure point. Fit the protection cover to the operating lever after greasing the bolt's thread and then attach the pad assembly, putting the friction spring in place and securing it with a well-greased adjusting nut and bolt. Fit the outer cover to

98 *It's unlikely that you'll have enough feeler gauges to measure the centralisation of the disc in the caliper. Therefore use a metal ruler or similar set quantity to pack out the space under the gauges. Measure each side in various places and evaluate.*

100 *Pivot pins have a habit of rusting up and so, as with all of the mechanism, need to be well-greased. Don't overtighten the pins. Fit the reaction plate and don't forget the lock tabs or the split pin through the adjusting bolt. If you leave some slack you can check the self-adjusting mechanism once more. Fit the brake pads retaining plate and brake pipes.*

the operating lever, put the bolt and the hinge pin through, securing the pin with a washer and greased split pin. If you work the mechanism it should click as the pads move closer to one another. It's essential to check this now because once the mechanism

ACTICAL CLASSICS RESTORATION PROJECT

01 *Our replacement shims were the individual type from the series three 'E' type and XJ. Originals are unavailable and less tidy anyway.*

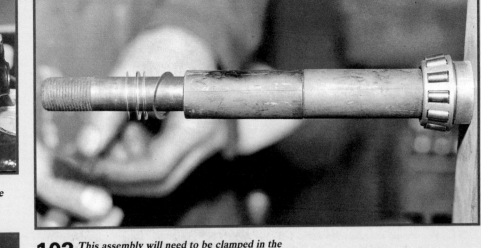

102 *This assembly will need to be clamped in the vice to set the end float.*

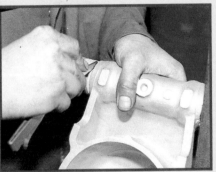

103 *Push and roll the carrier in and measure, then pull and roll out and measure again. Measurements should be dry and taken from the same position otherwise corrosion around the edge of the carrier may give misleading readings. The pre-load should be 0 to minus 2thou. Cleanliness is essential, too, and brake cleaner is ideal for this and for removing grease from the wife's carpet and clothes.*

104 *Push the splined hub as far as it will go and wobble it to settle the bearings. Zero the dial gauge and pull the hub out using screwdrivers that must be exactly opposite one another. Don't be content with one reading. Vary the screwdriver positions and take several readings. Our freeplay reading was 27thou.*

105 *Freeplay should be 2 to 6thou. This is a mean difference of 4thou. 27thou freeplay on the dial minus the mean difference of 4 leaves 23. We have a known 158thou on the other side. 158 minus 23 leaves 135. The closest shim to this is 136thou so this is fitted.*

is in the car it's very difficult to alter. There are split pins for the adjusting bolts but these should be left until the mechanism is on the caliper.

Slide the axle cage over the diff from the front and torque up the four top bolts to 75lb ft and wire the two pairs together. Roll over the cage and support it on some wood as the handbrake mechanism protrudes

from the cage.

Mount the fulcrum bracket, screw the bolts in finger-tight – note they're different lengths – then fit the fulcrum shaft through the cage and the bracket to ensure that everything moves freely. If it does, tighten up the bolts and wire them. Making sure that the inside of the distance tube is clean, put it in place next and then fit the inner fulcrum shaft after both it and the tube have been well-greased. A copper mallet may help. Before fitting the inner lower fulcrum it will be necessary to set the pre-load on the outer lower fulcrum carrier as described in caption 103.

Tap the outer races into both ends of the hub carrier. Mount the outer fulcrum shaft on to a section of angle iron, as shown, and fit the oil seal track, bearing, the spacing

tubes and a number of shims. Your old spacers should be two separate pieces whereas replacements are now one piece – this isn't a problem. We started with 35thou of shims located on the outer edge of the spacers. Incidentally, it makes no odds whether these are placed here or in between the two spacers. Fit the other bearing and oil seal. Place the hub carrier in position and use enough large packing washers to allow the outer nut to be tightened to 55lb ft. Measure and correct the free play.

We then turned our attention to the hub. We used a little grease on both the inner surface of the hub carrier and on the outer surface of the outer races (of the inner and outer bearings). These were then drifted into place. You should be able to tell when these races are fully home by listening. Alternatively, look through the grease plug to check. Clean the outer oil seal, pack it out with grease and tap into place or use a flat plate to drive it home in the hub carrier. Then push the outer oil seal track and the outer bearing on to the splined hub. Fit the splined hub to the carrier.

Although the free play should be measured dry, once everything has been placed in

PRACTICAL CLASSICS RESTORATION PROJECT

'E'type!

106 *You should mark which way the UJs come off the prop shaft so that they can be re-installed to work in the same plane and balance. This isn't so important on drive shafts. To fit the journal, remove the bearing caps. Lightly grease inside the yoke and press the cap part way home. Locate the journal and fit the other cap. Press both fully home in the vice. Using a socket, press the caps fractionally further to allow the circlip to fit both sides. Fit the grease nipple pointing away from the hub. Grease and ensure full movement.*

107

If the spring is painted use masking tape under the compressor lip to prevent scratching. Tighten and loosen the spring compressors evenly and make sure that the ends of the shock absorbers are parallel before releasing the pressure on the spring.

108 *Secure the right-hand-side of the mechanism and then adjust the left to fit without pressure. Centralise the adjuster and bolt into the captive nuts in the cage. The free movement of this whole mechanism is essential.*

109 *Make sure that the vice jaws are protected if the radius arm is painted. If you fit the rear bush first you can use the front bush to finish it in the vice if you don't have a large enough socket. This will not harm the steel bush. Fit the front bush the correct way around for the recess to take the cup under the body and fit it from the underside of the arm because of the lip on the top of the arm.*

the hub it cannot be removed to be packed. So lightly grease the inner bearing race – very sparingly. Then wipe over the top of the needle rollers lightly enough to prevent the the grease from going through. Once everything is moving the grease should flow in. Make sure there's plenty of grease on the oil seal and lightly smear the inner race of the bearing and the outer oil seal track. Too much grease will cause a heat build-up.

Put the inner bearing in place and clamp the hub assembly into a vice. To calculate the free play we have to know the exact distance between the top of the inner race and the splined hub. To determine this we used a disc (you can make one up) that had a circular instep (158thou in depth) the same width as the diameter of the splined hub while the overall cicumference of the disc was equal to that of the inner race as shown. You therefore place this disc face down on the bearing. As you tap the disc, it will drive the bearing into the hub and will only stop when the instep contacts the splined hub. It should be obvious when contact is made but, if you want to be sure, a smearing of engineer's blue on the two faces of the disc will colour the inner race and the splined hub when they are contacted by the two faces of the disc. You now know that the top of the inner race is 158thou away from the splined hub. After adjusting the freeplay as described in captions 104/105, tap the inner bearing oil seal into place. This has a leather edge that will require a light greasing.

Slide a greased oil seal track followed by the necessary shim on to the greased drive shaft. Slide the hub assembly on to the drive shaft ensuring that the hole for the split pin

on the shaft lines up with that on the hub. Drop a washer on to the stub and torque the castle nut up to 140lb ft. It's probable that you won't be able to get the required torque while the hub is in the vice and you may prefer to wait until the complete axle is fitted to the car. Our joint covers were rusted away and so were replaced with XJ parts. Secure with Jubilee clips. Grease the hub through the plug and turn the hub 20-30 times to work the grease in to the needle rollers. Fit the dust cover to the grease plug.

It's really a good idea to keep a list of such things as the shim sizes in the individual hubs. If your wheel bearings loosen up and need re-shimming, you can calculate the excess play, combine this with what you already know to be shimming the hub and find out what new shim is required without even stripping the hub. This way your car won't be off the road for weeks while you wait for the correct shim to arrive.

To finish off the wishbone, fit two bearings into each side of the lower inner fulcrum yoke with their etchings facing outwards so that they can be read from either side – the bearing cage is tapered. Don't worry if they seem a little loose; they should tighten up once the spacer has been pushed through. We then greased and fitted an inner thrust washer, oil seal, oil seal retainer and outer thrust washer to the inner and outer faces of both sides of the fulcrum yoke.

Using a 15mm copper tube as a dummy

we located the lower inner fulcrum on to its mount. Then we could slide the inner fulcrum shaft through the cage and the wishbone. Note that the bracket, for the radius arm on the wishbone, should face forwards.

Put the shock absorbers in place with their top bolts locating from the inside outwards and then fit the bottom bolt across the two. Don't forget to grease the tubes and bolts and use washers outside the bottom nuts.

Using the same disc shims that were taken off the car during the strip down (if possible), re-fit the drive shafts. This doesn't mean that they won't need adjusting but at least you should have a more accurate starting point. The correct locknuts should be used to secure the drive shaft to the disc. Nylocs are not recommended as the heat produced by hard braking may melt the nylon insert. For the time being it's worth fitting ordinary nuts because, if expensive locknuts need to be removed to make an adjustment to the shims, they will be ruined. Fit locknuts only when adjustments have been made.

Before fitting the hub to the wishbone, it will be necessary to bolt the radius arm to the wishbone. A special bolt with a thin head locates from inside the outer fulcrum mount and is largely inaccessible with the hub in place.

Another dummy shaft was used to locate the hub on to the lower outer fulcrum. The spacers, shims (that can now be fitted between the two spacers if you have the originals), bearings, oil seal retainers and oil seal tracks can now be fitted into place. slide the outer fulcrum shaft through the hub and tighten up the bolts. If there is still space in the fulcrum it will need to be shimmed out and the hub centralised.

Bolt the tie plate into position to complete the assembly.

NEXT MONTH
The front end of the car

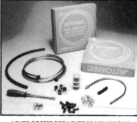

RACTICAL CLASSICS RESTORATION PROJECT

'E' type!

Part 10

The restoration has progressed a good way now as is obvious from the photographs. This month Philip Cooper brings us the latest build stage – the front suspension.

PRACTICAL CLASSICS RESTORATION PROJECT

'E' type!

The rear axle, the re-building of which was detailed in last month's issue, should now be fitted to the car. Once this is completed we can move to the front end, get the wheels on and bring the car back down to the ground.

After fitting the rear section of the petrol pipe underneath the offside of the car, beside the chassis leg, (as illustrated in picture 110) we can mount the axle. First the rearmost rear axle mounts should be bolted to the chassis legs because, with the axle in place, the inner face of these mounts will be inaccessible for bolt tightening. Don't forget the spacing shims that go with the mount. Ensure that all the brake pipes are complete then offer the axle into place. You will need to use a trolley jack with a piece of wood to spread the load in a similar way to when the axle was removed.

This job is obviously going to be easier with two people but, if you are doing it by yourself, the axle should be centralised and then slowly jacked into position, stopping at regular intervals to check that the axle is not fouling the bodywork or catching on anything else. When the central stud on the rear mount has located through the axle cage, fit a washer and wind the nut a few turns up the thread. With the forward mount secured on the axle cage it should be possible to line it up on the chassis leg. If you're using new mounts you may need to lever the holes into line with a screwdriver if they are slightly out but, if the difference between the mount and the chassis leg is too much, then something is amiss.

The bolts that locate through the mounts should be greased to stop them from rusting in and, if necessary, tapped through. Tighten the mounts. After greasing their cups, the radius arms may be positioned. Do not tighten them until the car is on the ground and supported in its normal plane unless you have setting links that will hold everything in a mid-laden position.

The rear anti-roll bar should be centralised across the rear bulkhead, fixed with the two locating brackets and rubbers and attached to the drop links which should have new bushes pressed into them. Following this, check that the propshaft fits in the tunnel. Finally fit the rubber bump stops.

With the axle fitted to the car the handbrake cable should be connected. This is a relatively straightforward procedure but you should make sure that, when you re-assemble the mechanism in the car, the warning light switch is adjusted correctly for it to work effectively. You should tighten the cable adjuster only as far as to remove any slack from the cable. If you have taken the time to set-up the calipers correctly, then this will be sufficient.

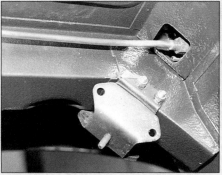

110 *You should fit this fuel pipe into place before the rear axle is offered up.*

111 *Don't forget the shims that go with the rear axle mounts.*

112 *This is how the bracket on the anti-roll bar mount should be positioned. The hole in the bracket will be used later when connecting up the brake hoses.*

Moving to the front of the car, the first part to be fitted should be the anti-roll bar. This is held to the frames in two places by an outer clamp, then a rubber bush (through which the bar passes), a backing plate and finally by an aluminium spacer.

The forwardmost lower fulcrum mount is next and this should be smeared with grease. Loosely fit the wishbone into place in approximately the correct position because it will be bunching up the rubber bush. Then grease and fit the rear mount into position. The bolts that secure both the front and the rear mounts should locate from the front of the car facing towards the back. We have used washers with the bolts although they were not originally fitted. Tighten up the fulcrum mounting bolts but leave the nuts at either end of the wishbone relatively loose until the car is on its wheels otherwise the bushes may become incorrectly stressed. Press the bushes into the anti-roll bar drop links and fit them on to the lower wishbone. It won't be necessary to connect these to the anti-roll bar until a much later stage when all the suspension is set-up.

113 *Remember to fit the small bolt that secures the torsion bar. Also fit the anti-roll bar drop link at this stage.*

114 *Once the ball joint has been correctly shimmed the spring should be fitted. With the spring in place for the final assembly it's going to be much more difficult to depress the cover plate to fit the circlip. Clamping will make this much easier . . .*

115 *Once you've fitted the rear mount to the top wishbone, tightening the nut should bring the mount into line with the holes on the frame.*

116 *Once the dust cover is fitted, check the movement of the joint once more.*

A suspension setting link (you can make one from the measurements given in the manual) should now be placed between the lower wishbone and the top of the 'picture frame' (where a shock absorber usually would be fitted).

To fit the torsion bar, you will need to clean and grease the splines on the torsion bar and the grooves on the lower wishbone and the rear bracket. Before assembly, it's as well to check that everything fits and moves smoothly when together. After putting the rear bracket on to the torsion bar, just locate the front end of the bar into the wishbone. Then fit the rear bracket to the chassis. Carefully turn the bar until all the splines line up at both ends. If the wishbone arms have been dismantled and re-fitted the wrong way around, you will have difficulty fitting the bar which, once located, will be stressed. With the bar in position fit the small bolt through the fulcrum arm to secure the bar.

Before fitting the upper wishbone the ball joint will need to be put in. Fit this joint and the ball pin socket. Keep packing it out with shims and fitting the cover plate and circlip until you find the correct quantity to hold the joint tight. Then remove 4thou and fit the spring and cover plate. Press them in to fit the circlip and then put the plastic washer and bleed nipple into place. Then grease and revolve the joint. Finally fit the plastic gaiter insert and the dust cover.

Put the upper wishbone into place using the shims that were taken off during dismantling. However, do remember that to use the old shims won't guarantee that the adjustment is correct, especially if you're not sure if the car was correctly set-up in the first place. You should still check the adjustment when the car is complete. Also don't confuse the backing plates, which locate on the rear of the mount, with the shims as the latter have one open and one closed hole through which the bolts go. Again, the inside of the wishbone mounts should be well-greased but don't allow any grease to remain on the rubber as this will cause contamina-

117 *It's going to be necessary to dismantle part of this assembly at a later stage when the engine is in place, so that the suspension can be set-up.*

PRACTICAL CLASSICS RESTORATION PROJECT

'E'type!

tion. With everything fitted, the bolts at either end of the wishbone should be slackened. Only tighten when the car is correctly laden.

Extend, then push back together, the shock absorbers several times to get the fluid moving. It will be necessary to jack-up the bottom wishbone, which may cause the car to rise as the engine is not in, to fit the shock absorbers. Don't forget the spacing sleeve on the bottom mount.

Uneven, restricted or notchy movements are all signs of wear on the stub axle ball joint. If in doubt replace it. Fit the Railko socket into the ball pin cup and bolt this with all the shims on to the stub axle. Tighten the bolts and keep adjusting the shims until the joint is held fairly tight. Then add a further 4-6thou of shims to give the correct freeplay. Tighten the four bolts, fold over the lock tabs and fit the plastic washer and grease nipple. Once the joint has been greased and well-worked, fit the plastic locator. This may need dipping in warm water to make it more pliable but be careful not to over-heat as this will cause it to lose shape. Fit the dust cap and nylon ring.

Bolt the stub axle to the lower wishbone and pull the upper wishbone down to fit the ball joint, which should be hand-tightened. Nylocs shouldn't be used at this stage as a certain amount of dismantling will be required to set the car's ride height once the engine is in and Nylocs can be used only once.

We then fitted the steering rack mounts to the frames. Offer up the rack and bolt it into place. You must ensure that the failsafes (the bolts that hold the rack if all else fails) are correctly located – they shouldn't be clamping down on to the rack. Fit the glass-fibre steering column cowl to the bulkhead. Move into the car and fit the lower column mounting bracket and the column to dash support. Make sure that the horn contact is insulated and fit the lock nut and upper section of the column. If the journals in the universal joints are worn replace them in the same way that we did the drive shaft UJs. Fit the upper UJ, centralise the rack and slide the lower UJ on to the column. Attach the column to the rack and feed it through the cowl on the bulkhead. Before clamping everything together put the steering wheel in place and work from lock to lock to check that everyting is central and that the indicators cancel. The UJ that connects to the steering rack is held by an Allen screw. This screw should be replaced if its head is even slightly damaged. It's advisable to use a ratchet to drive the screw home as it has to be tight and you don't want to run the risk of a second-rate key rounding any faces. You can now connect the tie rods to the rack. It's important to wind these on an even number of turns each side. We advise 20 turns each.

118 *This is what your final assembly should look like. There's no need to attach the drop link to the anti-roll bar.*

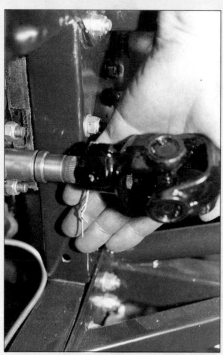

119 *A piece of wire attached to the steering rack shaft may be used to give a clear indication of how many turns you get out of the rack, thus allowing you to calculate the central point.*

120 *When you put the steering column back together ensure that the indicator cancelling mechanism/striker plate is located between the two indicator springs.*

Tap the outer races of the inner and outer bearings into the hub. If you are fitting a new splined hub, fit a water thrower to the inner side of the hub. Bolt the hub to the disc using special locking nuts, not Nylocs. Grease up the inner races of the bearings and put the inner bearing into the hub followed by a greased oil seal. After checking that the oil seal track on the stub axle (it should already be there) is not damaged, slide the assembly on to the stub axle. Make a mental note of where the split pin holes are because, with all the grease in there, you're not going to be able to see. Fit the outer bearing into the hub. Fit the D washer and the castellated nut (hand-tight) followed by the grease nipple and the split pin. Offer up and fit the brake calipers. For convenience you can attach the tie rod ends to the steering arm on the stub axle. This shouldn't be tightened at this stage but will at least allow you to steer the car around the workshop.

NEXT MONTH
Replacing the servo and
fitting-up the doors.

RACTICAL CLASSICS RESTORATION PROJECT

'E'type!

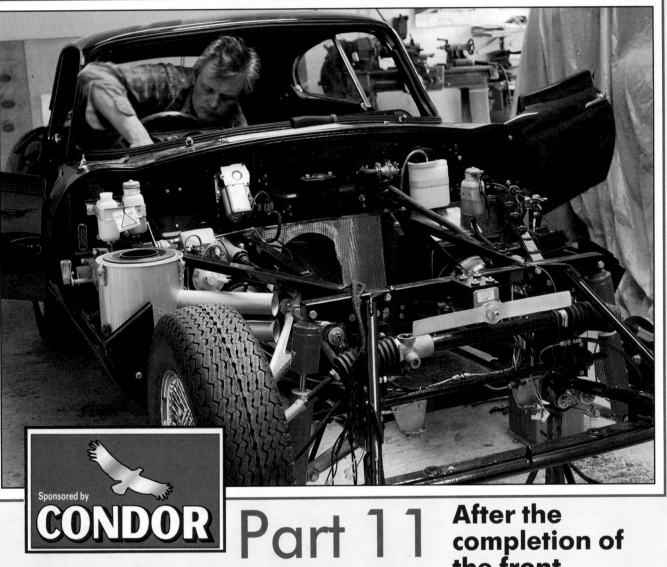

Part 11

After the completion of the front suspension last month Philip Cooper reports as Colin Ford tends to a number of smaller jobs around the car.

PRACTICAL CLASSICS RESTORATION PROJECT

'E'type!

121 When stripping the servo put a bar across two of the nuts and turn in an anti-clockwise direction to release.

122 Remove this securing pin to release the diaphragm support.

123 Offering up the transfer pipes to the outside of the bulkhead will give a better idea of their correct location. Old Jag heaters are notoriously inefficient and pipe insulation will help to maintain temperature.

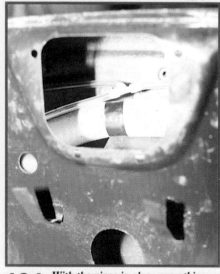

124 With the pipes in place everything else may be put into the bulkhead box section. Note the red oxide.

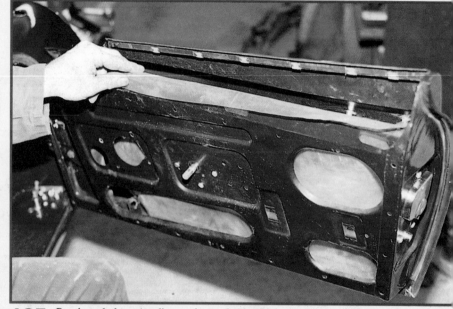

125 Put the polythene (medium or heavy duty), which must cover all the apertures, in place and secure the door release mechanism through this.

126 With the door release mechanism in place, the window winder may be located and secured.

It's now time to start rummaging through your boxes of parts and searching out the various ancillary components that were packed away at the beginning during the car's initial strip-down. All will need to be examined and, if suitable, re-conditioned and put back on the car.

In our case Colin began with the servo. First it was drained and then clamped into a vice with its rear end facing upwards. Two nuts were put on to each of the three studs with the flats on each pair lined up. Using a screwdriver, gently flex each lip overlap to ensure that any corrosion is broken and use WD40 to help at this stage. Place a crowbar in between two of the bolts and turn in an anti-clockwise motion.

If you cannot get any movement using this method don't get carried away and force it, just take it to a garage with a specialist tool. If the top does move, however, turn it

until the lips line-up. Undo the nuts on the studs and lift off the casing. Pull the black rubber diaphragm up and over the centre circle. Then, having removed the servo from the vice, hold it horizontally and push in the

black diaphragm support to release its secu ring clip and allow it to be removed, reveal ing the spring.

Next turn the servo the other way up and knock the locking tabs off the three nuts

74

128 *These shims adjust the door frame angle.*

127 *Fit the frame and window into the door. Note the location of the window in the frame.*

Take the nuts out and lift off the vacuum cylinder shell and remove the gasket.

One very common fault that you should look for is a damaged rear seal which will allow fluid to leak into the servo. Apart from a loss of braking efficiency, which may not be very apparent at first, one obvious symptom is pungent white smoke from the exhaust. This results from fluid in the servo being drawn into the induction pipes and into the engine.

Undo the bolt for the inlet connection (feed from the reservoir) and remove the piston. A rod can then be inserted into the cylinder which, provided it's not seized, will release the pressure on the stop pin in the hole. Extract the pin and, using a pair of long-nosed pliers, remove anything else that's left in the slave cylinder body.

Remove the front outlet connection union and lift out the plastic trap valve and spring. Clean and inspect the bore. Assuming there is no damage, everything can then be put back together simply by reversing the procedure.

Now we have reached an appropriate stage for the transfer pipes and windscreen wiper mechanisms to be re-fitted to the bulkhead. But before this is done Colin advises that the bulkhead be treated with red oxide and then Waxoyl. Although this region of the car is not particularly prone to rusting it still makes good sense to carry out fairly thorough rustproofing.

Once Colin had insulated them, all the transfer pipes were put in to the box section of the bulkhead. You will probably remember how difficult it was to remove these pipes because of the restricted access. Well, the bad news is that re-fitting them is even harder due to the new insulation around

them. You should locate the lowest pipe first and work upwards. If you have forgotten which pipes go where, you can get a good idea of their location by offering them up to their apertures from the outside of the bulkhead.

With the transfer pipes riveted into place the windscreen washers were next to be fitted. The plastic 1/8in pipe should be measured up to length leaving a couple of inches spare for bends etc. Too much slack will foul the wiper mechanism. Cut the pipe just off centre and trial fit the washer jets. Provided the fit is correct then fix the jets to the bulkhead. Your original jets probably will have had wing nuts underneath. While these are easier to tighten they are prone to working loose, especially when you clean around them. It's likely that your new jets will be supplied with ordinary nuts. These, too, will be susceptible to coming loose and it's therefore a good idea to use spring washers as we did. Set the jet heads parallel to the bulkhead.

As far as the wipers are concerned for ease of fitting you should unbolt the wheel boxes at both ends of the mechanism. Put the mechanism into the box section of the bulkhead and locate the parking adjuster. This will be a rather fiddly job due to restricted access and because this section is now full of pipes not to mention the Waxoyl that's going to make everything slippery. Back in the November issue I suggested you persuaded someone with small hands to help out and the same applies here too.

With the mechanism in place, re-bolt the wheel boxes, locate them through the bodywork and fit the rubbers, escutcheons and bolts. Ensure that everything moves freely and that none of the splines is worn. Don't over-tighten the escutcheons because the threads are only thin. Finger-tight will be sufficient. From this stage you can carry out further Waxoyling if you wish.

Colin then fitted the door A and B post seals. With these in place the chances of chipping the paintwork with the door is less likely. However, with the new seals in place, you may find it difficult to shut the door. This is not unusual but if you shut the door tight then the seals should settle in. The door may sit slightly proud for a while but should come into line as the seals compress. If the second catch won't take don't be tempted to to slam the door and certainly

PRACTICAL CLASSICS RESTORATION PROJECT

'E'type!

don't apply any force to the door skins as these will simply bend. If necessary, adjust the door catch so that it does take. After some time the seals will settle and the catch may be adjusted again back to its original position.

Colin then fitted the door handle, applied self-adhesive sound deadening to the inside of the doorskin and treated the whole area with Waxoyl. If the Waxoyl is thinned with white spirits it will flow better into the seams to give improved sealing. Also don't forget to spray up inside the top lip.

Adjust the pin on the push button so that it releases the catch when the button is depressed. Give the mechanism a good greasing and make sure that the interior door handle works. Careful adjustment at this stage will save a lot of time and embarrassment later. If the interior door handle doesn't work properly there will be a good chance that the door will lock itself when it slams shut, so be warned!

Stripping the internals out of the door is fairly straightforward. Once everything has been removed it should be cleaned-up and inspected to make sure that it's all in good working order. It can then be fitted back into the door.

Start re-fitting the door by putting the water-resistant polythene sheet into place. As the water runs down the window and into the door, this sheet should channel it down to the bottom of the door where it can escape through the drain holes. Cut the polythene to the correct shape and glue it in place at the top of the door.

If you're re-using your old doors you should take particular note of the drainage tray at the top of the door near the hinges. This is prone to rusting and might well need to be replaced. Cut and stick a new rubber channel into the door frame and slide the window in. It should run smoothly but may seem slightly tight at first. Once again things should improve with use. Don't forget to fit the weather strips either.

To fit the window frame the glass will need to be slightly down otherwise it might foul the weather strip as it slides the last few centimetres into place. Be sure to see that the weather strip locates into its correct position at the front. Put the two mounts into the bottom of the door and note that the front mount is shorter than the rear. Keep the polythene pulled up and out of the way and locate the winding mechanism under the glass. With this complete carefully pull the polythene down. If the polythene gets torn at this stage, you will have to take everything out again and start from square one. Lift the mechanism into place and push the winder mount through the aperture and the polythene, which must be in the correct position.

Line-up the holes around the winder spring and locate at least one of the screws. Then bring the bracket to the rear of the

129 *Put the screw through the frame and secure it with a bracket underneath.*

130 *Drill the holes and fit the data plate before fixing the fuel bowl into place.*

131 *The heat reflector/sound deadener may be fixed into the transmission tunnel. You will be glad of this minor detail during hot weather as it prevents some heat from being transmitted to the cockpit.*

door opening handle. Push the four studs through the polythene (again making sure that it's properly pulled down) and secure it with four nuts. These should be locking nuts but we shall come back to this at a later date. Locate the frame to the bottom rear mount with a well-greased bolt. Locate the forward mount and hand-tighten both. Be careful when working the glass through the new rubber guide, especially if the glass is new, because it might rip it.

Put the six screws through the frame and place the three brackets underneath. Using the shims take it to the fullest extent. This is done for the same reason that we shimmed out the bonnet. Therefore, when the door is closed it will be least likely to foul anything as the frame will be at its greatest outward angle. You can then reduce the adjustment from here to get a correct fit.

With all the rubbers and mechanism fitted, the door will obviously be heavier. Its seating on the hinges will therefore be affected and you should close the door very carefully and paying particular attention to the front edge. You may well find that this now catches so further adjustment will be required. Having fitted the chrome B post it will be possible to adjust the door frame, by varying the quantity of shims, so that it fits flush with the rest of the bodywork.

To finish of this month numerous smaller items such as the horn mount, brake union pipe, alternator warning light relay (on the nearside of the bulkhead) and the clutch pipes were all be fitted and the brake hoses were connected to the rear.

NEXT MONTH
Trimming the interior

'E' type!

Part 12

After last month's 'odd jobs' Colin Ford now gets back inside the car to carry out rustproofing and re-trimming. Report by Philip Cooper.

PRACTICAL CLASSICS RESTORATION PROJECT

'E' type!

With various smaller jobs around our 'E' type completed, we can make a start on the interior. However, before the trim is fitted into place, the monocoque will need to be thoroughly rustproofed even though much of it is already protected with seam sealers, red oxide and a good coating of paint.

To rustproof the car, Waxoyl or a similar substance should be injected into the monocoque. To achieve this an air line is ideal but, failing that, you can use a pump-up insecticide type sprayer.

Colin carried out all the work from inside the car and started with the sills. The sprayer was inserted in the holes that run along the length of the inner sill with larger apertures in the box sections of the A and B post which should also be thoroughly treated at this stage.

He then sprayed inside the rear wings, again gaining access through apertures that can be found on the inside of the car. Also in the same region were the petrol filler box and the area in the boot into which the petrol pump locates. To complete the rear of the car Colin tackled the box sections behind the number plate lights and inside both the rear door and the tonneau section.

We advise that, where possible, you should also attempt to Waxoyl the chassis members, chassis rails and the crossmembers inside the car (across the floors and behind the seats).

Dealing with the front end will complete the rustproofing programme and, to do this, it was necessary for Colin to coat inside all the apertures and box sections (especially the headlamps) in the bonnet.

Because it's unlikely that the spray will be able to contact all the surface area he backed-up his efforts by jacking up the front end of the car and leaving it thus for one or two days. This allowed the Waxoyl to flow to the rear. To aid this flow, and to encourage the Waxoyl to seep into the tightest of seams, Colin's first application was thinned down in solution with 30 per cent of white spirits. The rear of the car was then jacked-up to give flow to the forwardmost parts of the inner sills etc. After another one or two days the car was levelled once again and a second 'pure' application of Waxoyl was injected. The same jacking procedure followed to complete the rustproofing.

You can expect to use at least a gallon of Waxoyl on the body. Certainly a greater amount wouldn't do any harm but, if you're going to do it at all, to economise on your quantities would nullify your efforts.

It's likely that the Waxoyl will take a good couple of months to dry completely. Even then, though, it's possible that if the car

Before any of the dash is fitted a piece of material of this size will need to be positioned between where the cant rail and dashtop will fall. If this is not fitted the body colour will show through a small gap at the side of the dash. Although this might not be such a problem with dark coloured cars, on light cars it would be rather blatant.

With the headlining complete and the cant rail in place you should cover and fit the sunvisors, rear mirror and interior light etc.

If your boot floor/spare wheel cover needs replacing you should use seven-ply wood. This can be cut using the original as a template. Stick a thin layer of foam to this followed by a covering of vinyl.

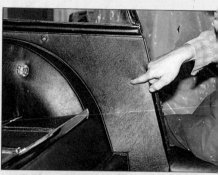

With all the interior panels in place lift the front luggage board to right angles and mark where the chrome stop will need to be positioned. Rivet it in place.

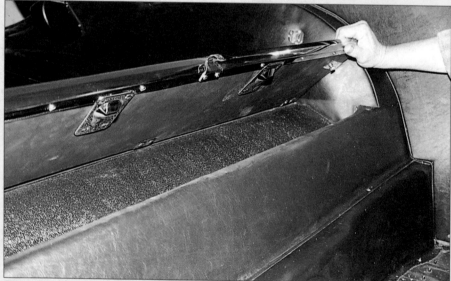

The hinged luggage stops (two) on the forward luggage board can fit in only one place. The remaining luggage strips (on both the front and rear boards) may be accurately positioned by making them equidistant from each other in the remaining space. Even if they are accurately separated only secure them with one screw at first and then step back to ensure that it looks correct.

were left out in the hot summer sun (provided we get one) the Waxoyl may liquidise again and come through the seams. It's therefore unwise to leave your car on a nice drive until you know how it's going to behave for fear of causing costly or embarrassing damage!

With the rust prevention complete, Colin could consider re-fitting the trim. The car was painted in British Racing Green as this was how it left the factory. The interior, therefore, also will be trimmed as per original specification which was black.

Because the old leather was incomplete

and damaged we acquired a new set from Barry Hankinson (Tel: 0989 65789). However, before we started to fit this a couple of other jobs in areas that won't be accessible once the trim is in place had to be completed.

First the wiring needed to be routed around the car. The main bulk of the loom is positioned across the length of the bulkhead behind the dash. While he was there Colin also fixed the four fuse holders into place and the relay for the lights which needs to be screwed into the bulkhead just right of centre. The wires for the indicator switches

PRACTICAL CLASSICS RESTORATION PROJECT

Push the rubber seal in around the edge of the aperture and trim off any excess.

Drill the holes through for the catch and then fit with self-tappers. Don't forget the wedge-shaped packing piece.

Once the rear door is in place the hinge covers may be positioned and screwed into place.

Gradually replace all the screws to secure the screen.

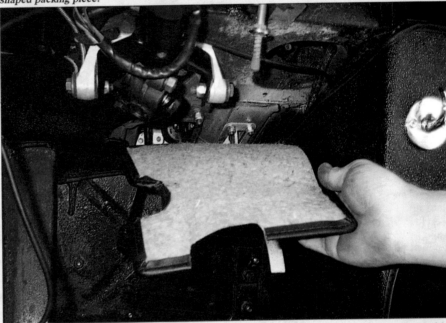

The Hardura fits to the side of the footwells and the underside of the dash. It is held in place with chrome self-tappers and cup washers, as are the chrome finishers.

were then connected and the cables for the choke, heater controls and the speedometer were all fed through the bulkhead and into the engine bay. Colin then lay the rest of the wiring in place.

The loom feeds down both sills and it was necessary to use some stiff wire (or a rod) to guide it through some of the box sections. On the nearside, part of the loom will need to be connected to the wiring that supplies the rear interior light. The rest should run to the back of the car. Once it was in place Colin connected the rear lights, the number plate lights and the reversing lights. Also at the rear on the offside are the wires for the petrol pump. Connect these now.

It's highly important at this stage to remember the wire to the handbrake switch. This comes from the offside loom, travels behind the driver's seat, across the transmission tunnel and plugs into the switch below the handbrake. Colin also laid the wiring to the doors' switches for the courtesy lights.

Following this the three binnacles (faces) of the dash were offered into place. Then the plastic mould around the rear door aperture was positioned.

When fixing the headlining into place either an aerosol or tinned glue should be used. Whichever your choice follow the manufacturer's instructions and steer clear

of slapping it on haphazardly as it could soak through the material and spoil the finish.

The centre of the lining was placed on the roof first and the material was gradually smoothed and worked outwards. Around the edges there should be an excess of material. This needs to be trimmed down as much as is practical but ideally leaving at least ¼in. Trim off the excess and tuck-in the rest. To complete the headlining cover the four remaining side sections – the joint cover between cant rails, down the fixed parts of the cant rail sides, and across the back.

Following this Colin filled the indentations on the rear wings (strengthening moulds) with a foam template that will give a flush finish. Tinned glue was then applied to the inner wings and their covers were positioned, flattened out and allowed to dry. Note that the covers will probably require some trimming.

While aerosols give accurate applications of strong glue they are not always appropriate as the glue can set too quickly. Tinned glue, however, usually takes longer to set and will therefore allow for the material to be re-positioned once it's in place to give the smoothest and most accurate fit.

Colin then progressed to cover the lower cross panel behind the seats after which a

foam backing was glued to the sills, allowing the sill covers to be fitted. Cover the support cross rail and position it on to the lower cross panel. Before fixing it in place, though, the boot floor and forward hinged luggage board were put into position. The pins either side of the hinged luggage board should locate into holes in the support cross rail. Correct alignment for this can be checked before anything is secured. Rivet the support cross rail into place – two rivets either side hold it to the inner wings and a further two at the front rivet down into the lower cross panel. Following a logical progression, Colin could then fix both the forward side panels into the car and then the tonneau panel at the rear of the boot. After that the rear side panels were fitted.

The trunking that fits underneath the dash on the nearside of the car covering the wiring that leads in to the bulkhead was then put into position and secured. If you're fitting an aerial in the original position (front offside) this needs to go in now. Following that the Hardura side panels are fitted inside the footwell and over the bonnet pulls. Colin continued by fitting the cant rails, not forgetting the chrome finishers at the ends.

That completed the interior trimming for now so Colin turned his attention to the fitting of the side windows. To start, the rub-

'E'type!

ber seal was pushed into the channel around the window aperture. A blunt object should be used to do this and, although the seal can be glued into place, it's not strictly necessary.

Colin then put a seal into the side window frame, added lubrication and eased the glass into place. The front strut was then added which, once the four screws (two top and two bottom) had been put in, completed this assembly. To fit the window Colin put one screw in the base of the hinge plate, offered the side window into place and wound the screw into the chrome B post about 1 1/2 turns. Gradually more screws were added until they were all in place. Before tightening these screws, he closed the window to check the fit. After tightening, the window catch was attached to the frame. Its other end then needed to be screwed to the inside of the car. To get the positioning for this correct, Colin held the window closed and locked over the catch. It was then possible to see exactly where the catch would need to be secured to ensure a good fit when the window is closed. The catch was held in this position and opened to give the drill access to the screw holes. Holes were drilled and screws put in to secure. If the chrome gutter strip is in place at this stage you can also make sure that the fitted window doesn't catch on it when it is opened and closed.

Returning to the trim at the rear of the car, Colin put the upper casing on to the back door and the short casing above the door catch.

If you're re-covering either of the larger casings be very careful if you cut triangles out of the material to give a flat finish where the casing bends in towards the windscreen aperture with the door contours. These cuts can easily split up the material so that they are visible. Remember also that the screen rubber will pull the vinyl down which will also lead to the cuts becoming visible if they have not been made shallow enough. Colin offered up the lower casing, again taking great care over any trimming or cutting.

Stick and clip the lower casing around the window aperture. Once the window is in you will be able to poke the heater element wires through the door and the vinyl. It will then be possible to get your hand under the casing to join the bullet connecters to the main loom wires. Push the rest of the clips into place to finish off the lower casing. Hold the window rubber into place to check that everything fits.

Fit the catch and the rear seal and trial open and shut the door. When everything was found to be in good working order Colin fitted the covers over the hinges and over the catch.

Connect all the gauges and switches etc. The upper Harduras were then fitted up underneath the dash. On the driver's side this comes in two parts as it has to go round the

After fitting the cant rails put the chrome finishers in place and mount the leather passenger-side grab handle.

The last stage this month is to re-fit the dashtop. It's a lot more convenient to leave the front screen out while trimming the interior and fitting the dash. This is especially true for the home restorer working alone.

steering column. Colin then put the under dash scuttle panels into place. This should be done before the dashtop is fitted so that you can see down into the dash, making it easier to locate the various screws and bolts. All the gauges and switches etc. were then connected.

Colin decided that our dashtop needed recovering. To do this he unscrewed and removed the air vent covers and took off the clips holding the cover at the rear of the dash. The dashtop was then removed from the steel support frame. The new cover was placed over the steel support frame and located in its final position. Trim the front edge of the cover to the steel frame by warming the rigid plastic to make it pliable and then stick it down with a good impact adhe-

sive. Warm the plastic on the opposite edge, turn it over the steel lip, and re-secure with the clips. The air-vent bezels (re-paint in matt black if required) were then re-fitted and the existing screw holes located. Colin then ran a pencil inside the vents to mark the cut-outs. After using a sharp scalpel to do this the vents were replaced and the completed dashtop was fitted to the car. It's worth noting that only a gentle heat should be used and excessive pressure must not be used when bending.

NEXT MONTH
More trim and details.

PRACTICAL CLASSICS RESTORATION PROJECT
'E'type!

Sponsored by
CONDOR

Part 13

This month Colin Ford finishes a couple more jobs on the car before Philip Cooper goes over to Metalock to cover the repair of our 'E' type engine block.

PRACTICAL CLASSICS RESTORATION PROJECT

'E' type!

In last month's issue we were in Colin Ford's workshop (CF Autos, 5 South Road, Erith, Kent. Tel: 0322 346584) finishing off some of the car's trimwork. Once we've completed that this month the car will be ready for the installation of its engine.

However, before we put the engine in or even consider re-building it, it will need to be repaired. As you may remember, our 'E' type was bought in a poor state. The engine had already been dismantled and there was a rather large crack at the top of the block. As if this wasn't enough there was also evidence that repairwork had been carried out in the lower sections of the block. So things didn't look too promising for the future of that particular casting.

However, Metalock Ltd, at Metalock House, Crabtree Manorway, Belvedere, Kent DA17 6AB (Tel: 081-311 4040) said they could repair our block and so it was taken to them for the work. Before I cover that, however, there are two more jobs to be done on the car.

The first task is to fit the front and rear windscreens. These are a very tight fit, especially with new rubbers. Satisfactory completion is therefore rather hard (it's adequately covered in the workshop manual) and unless you're particularly confident we would suggest you use a professional fitter. Even Colin took this option as the fitter's charge was more reasonable than that involved in replacing a broken screen. This is especially true if you're fitting the laminated type of rear screen with the heater element in it. If you break this that's your lot as they are no longer available.

However, I should point out that fitting a window in the rear may cause the tailgate to flex and change shape. Therefore be exceptionally careful when you open or close it for the first time as the edges may catch on the body and remove the paint.

We then replaced the petrol tank. As this has to slide through the cut-out in the rear stiffener, and is particularly tight, we put some cloth down here and in the boot floor to prevent the paint from being scratched. The fuel pipe was then connected.

With work on the car finished for the time being I can now bring you the details of how our block was repaired – not something you should attempt at home!

This technique of metalwork repair was initially used in the marine world for repairing ships etc. It became an established method many years ago and its relative simplicity has fended off technological advances over the years so it is successfully used still in a wide range of applications today.

As this is a fairly time-consuming process, for our purposes we are only going to cover the repair of the first section of the crack only as far as the engine numbers. The rest

144 *The more cost-effective method of installing the windscreens, unless you're particularly confident, may well be to use a professional fitter.*

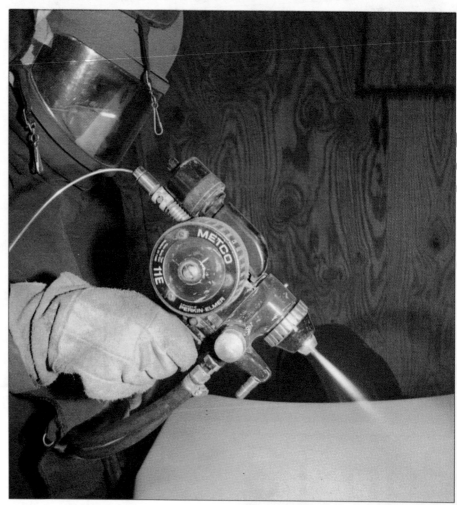

145 *For experimental purposes we had our petrol tank zinc-coated by Classic Engineering, 503 Southbury Road, Enfield, Middlesex EN3 4JW, (Tel: 081 805 5534). Although this is a rather expensive process it is claimed to give prolonged protection against rust.*

of the crack will be sealed in the same manner, the only difference being that working along the numbers without obstructing or de-facing them requires extreme accuracy and a good deal of patience.

146 *After using a centre punch, numbers of holes were drilled along the length of the crack at regular intervals.*

PRACTICAL CLASSICS RESTORATION PROJECT

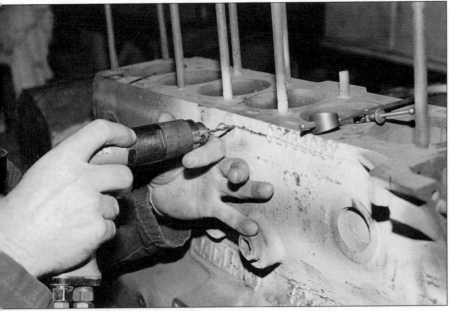

147 *The length of the repair was equally sectioned with a pair of dividers. A slightly larger hole was then drilled on the line which indicates the end of each division.*

148 *The centre pin on this special block locates into these larger drill holes. This block was held secure while further holes were drilled either side of the crack (four holes and six holes respectively) giving a line of holes at right angles*

149 *The studs that were then placed between these lines had flat heads which snapped off, due to the pressure, when they were fully home. Any heads then left above the suface of the block were chiselled flat. These studs will prevent the engine from flexing outwards on the crack. Note the use of red jointing paste as we are tapping into the water jacket.*

150 *A thin chisel was then used to make a slot along the key holes. Keys were then positioned and tapped in. Because they are made of a nickel and steel alloy they will expand, when heated, at the same rate as the engine.*

151 *The keys were then cross peaned (special tool with hammering action) until flush with the block except for the centre key which is to have a stud placed next to it and therefore cannot be flattened just yet. Further holes were then tapped between the keys and the first stud.*

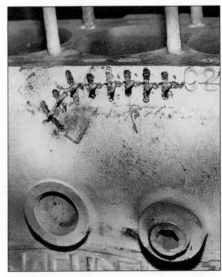

152 *These studs should be fitted so that they just touch the key on their one side and the stud on their other. If this fit is not achieved the fracture no doubt will leak again. Drill the stud in until the head snaps.*

PRACTICAL CLASSICS RESTORATION PROJEC

'E' type!

153 *All the tops were now cross peined with this tool. As the heads flatten out over the surface they overlap each other and make a seal.*

154 *All the studs and keys cross peined.*

155 *After grinding down the surface the repair is only just visible*

156 *This is the block completely repaired, numbers and all. To the unsuspecting eye the crack and repair are not visible and once the block has been painted it will look as if there never was anything wrong with this engine.*

The purpose of running keys at right angles to the fracture is to prevent it from separating further which will be particularly critical when the head is bolted down. It also returns the strength to the block. The other point to note is that the keys alternate

between 5 and 7 holes to act as a safeguard if the block ever came under pressure, thus preventing the stress from finding an equal level of weakness in the metal along which it could split.

After this treatment the block was pressure tested with air. Soapy water was then added to see if any bubbles appeared along the length of the repair. As they didn't the job was considered to be good.

In the lower section of the block there was further evidence of damage. On inspection this was confirmed and it is thought that the block here had cracked before. It had been welded up and, although the job was neat, it wasn't effective (probably done by an inexperienced cast welder) and leaking continued. We therefore sent the block off for the second part of its repair.

Another company carried out this repair in the form of ceramic sealing. This would cast off any doubts about the lower damage and, although it didn't need it, act to strengthen the top repair further.

For this process the block was thoroughly flushed out. Cleaning out the block is also a pre-build requirement for anyone with a good block. At home this is done by removing the core plugs and using a blunt instrument to scrape off and loosen-up any debris or corrosion. The block should then be flushed with water by inserting a garden hose in each of the plug holes.

A hot solution was poured into the block which was then pressurised to around 35psi. (As the normal running pressure of these Jaguar engines is below 10psi any other weaknesses would now show up). Under pressure the solution would be forced into even the smallest fissure and once, cooling had taken place, should make a perfect seal.

NEXT MONTH
The engine rebuild

PRACTICAL CLASSICS RESTORATION PROJECT

'E' type!

Sponsored by
CONDOR

Part 14

Last month we detailed the repair of our engine block. With that exercise completed Philip Cooper takes up the story as the power plant is rebuilt.

PRACTICAL CLASSICS RESTORATION PROJECT

'E' type!

Prior to the rebuild the engine was sent away to Rovercraft at Unit One, Progress Estate, Parkwood, Maidstone, Kent ME15 9YH (Tel: 0622 687070), where it was to be machined. It had been decided that our British Racing Green car should also be environmentally 'green'. Therefore, when the head was reconditioned, it was fitted with bronze valve guides, stainless steel inlet and exhaust valves and high nickel content inlet and exhaust valve seat inserts. Rovercraft also balanced all the rotating parts together with the pistons and con rods.

All the components then returned to Colin Ford's workshop where they were thoroughly cleaned. Colin did this by removing the oil gallery plugs and using generous amounts of cleaning agent. All the galleries were then blown through with an air line and the plugs replaced with copper washers. The rest of the engine and the bores etc. were then thoroughly cleaned, after which the block was painted in its original black. Cleaning should be done with non-fluffy rags or swabs.

Beginning the rebuild, Colin fitted the top rear oil seal into its housing (ring dowl). The seal is made of asbestos rope which ideally should be soaked overnight in oil. We advise that this is done, especially if you're not sure when the engine will first be run, as it will prevent the seal from drying out. Colin used Hylomar sealing paste as a precautionary measure because the oil shouldn't come up to this level anyway.

With the engine inverted on the bench Colin could fit the top shells (with the oil tracks). There is a locating lug on the bottom of the shells which will cause them to overlap if they were fitted incorrectly so you can't really go wrong. All the shell surfaces were liberally oiled and the crank positioned.

He then oiled the crank journals and the main bearing caps (with the bottom shells in place). The centre cap was fitted with a standard end float washer and then bolted into place. By pushing the crank forward and rotating it the end float could be measured. This should read between 4thou-6thou. Colin pushed a pair of feeler gauges into the gap either side of the centre journal to make the measurements – the two readings should be equal. Following this all the caps were tightened and the locking tabs were bent up. Don't forget to fit the oil pipe mounts.

The next stage was for Colin to fit the con rods to the pistons. On some models there is a tiny hole about half way up the con rod. Make sure that this hole faces the exhaust side of the engine when the arrow on the top of the piston is facing towards the front of the car. If you have difficulty fitting the

157

Push the asbestos seal into the ring dowl from either end. The seal will either bow in the middle or protrude from both ends. Don't trim this but clamp the dowl into a vice and roll the seal until it fits in.

158 *Bolt the ring dowl to the block using the shorter of the three bolts in the centre. Note that the two end shells are the largest, the middle is slightly smaller and the remaining four are the smallest of all.*

gudgeon pins you should heat the pistons by standing them in boiling water for about 20 minutes. However, don't allow the level of the water to come up as high as the rings. Once in place the gudgeon pins are secured with circlips which should be new even if you're only overhauling the engine. Make sure the rings are offset against one another so that none of the rings gaps is in line.

If you're fitting new rings to old pistons you should check the ring gaps. Compress the ring by hand, put it in the bore and use a piston to push the ring deeper. Then measure the gap. It should read between 15thou and 20thou for this engine.

Fit the rings to the pistons, compress them and use the wooden handle of a hammer to tap the piston gently until you know the rings are about to go into the block. Then use a slightly heavier tap to push all the rings into the engine in one movement.

159 *Fill the tracks in the shells with oil before fitting the crankshaft.*

PRACTICAL CLASSICS RESTORATION PROJECT

160 *Take out the plugs in the journals and clean inside. There may be a lot of dirt here especially if the crank has been ground. Once the plug is back in use a blunt chisel to pein (burr) the edge over so that it won't undo.*

161 *A standard crankshaft thrust washer should be fitted initially.*

162 *Don't forget to bolt all the appropriate oil pipe mounting brackets into place.*

163 *Fit the piston so that the tiny hole on the con rod (which spills out oil and lubricates the bore) faces the exhaust side (not all models have this hole) and ensure that the arrow on top of the piston faces to the front of the car. Liberally oil the piston and the bore before it is fitted and again check that the rings are offset against each other.*

164 *Use a ring compressor and fit the piston by gently tapping with the wooden handle of a hammer.*

165 *Position pistons one and six at top dead centre. Put the distributor drive gear in at this orientation and fit the thrust washer. Tap the cog into place and secure with a lock tab and bolt.*

166 *Tighten up the mechanism and measure the end float by pulling the cog outwards. If it measures more than 6thou replace the gear cog.*

167 *Prime the oil pump before it is fitted.*

When doing this you must make sure that the ring compressor is positioned squarely on top of the cylinder block. If there is any gap one of the rings may slip out slightly and break as it goes into the bore. You would be none the wiser until you started the engine – very demoralising. It's also a good idea to put some rag around the end of the con rod when you're fitting the pistons to avoid any

168 *Fit the oil pump using a coupling link, then begin to fit the oil pipes.*

metal to metal contact.

After each piston has been fitted, rotate the crankshaft to ensure free movement. There is no particular order for fitting the pistons. The big end bearings were oiled and connected to the journal.

PRACTICAL CLASSICS RESTORATION PROJECT

'E'type!

The pistons and rods should have a number stamped on them for identification – they were weighed and balanced as pairs and so should always be kept together. Also the cup for the rod, that will also be numbered, should be fitted in such a way that it reads the same way around as that in the rod. This is how they would have been assembled when they were set-up.

After fitting one of our pistons and bolting the con rod to the crankshaft, we had difficulty turning the engine. However, as we had turned the engine after each individual piston had been fitted, we knew that the last fitted was the one at fault. After removing the cap Colin found that the shell was shiny on one side only which suggested that the con rod wasn't quite aligned properly. The piston was taken out and then re-fitted after which everything moved smoothly.

If the worm gear isn't already fitted do this now – it just slides into the keyway. Before setting up the distributor drive (as described in caption 166) we fitted a new distance drive bush. The old unit had been damaged because the block had obviously been dragged across the floor a few times since it had been taken out of the car a few years ago.

Before fitting, the oil pump was primed by filling it with oil and rotating its shaft. It could then be mounted once Colin had placed a coupling on the distributor drive. A dowl bolt and lock tab were then used to secure the pump. Following this O rings were put into the pick-up and feed apertures. The pick-up pipe was then attached to the pump. This must be a snug fit. The other dowl bolt was then fitted as was the ordinary bolt that locates between the two dowls. After the pick-up pipe had been bolted to the centre bracket the feed pipe was fitted using Hylomar gasket seal.

Colin then inspected and prepared the timing chains. If the chains have a connecting link in them this may be undone and the chains removed. Otherwise you will have to strip the mechanism by releasing the circlip and removing the four nuts and shakeproof washers. The short chain goes around the bottom cogs while the long one goes around the top. Once the mechanism is stripped you should clean up any areas that are dirty.

Colin re-assembled the mechanism with the chains in place. If you have linked chains they should be fitted so that the rounded edges travel in the forward direction. Before the tensioner was fitted Colin put a small but important cone-shaped filter into the oil gallery beside which the tensioner will be positioned. The tensioner was then put in and turned slightly so that the adjusting spring mechanism released. If you have the older Allen key type, again this should be turned slightly but never force it into the chain. With the engine upright the slippers were fitted with the bottom two just coming into contact with the chain. Finally this month

169 *This is what the assembly should look like. Before fitting the sump, pump oil down the feed pipe and rotate the engine. This will put oil in all the correct places so that when the engine first turns none of the bearing surfaces etc. will be dry.*

170 *Once the chains have been taken out of their housing they can be inspected. If you hold them horizontally in front of you they shouldn't sag too much. The other way is to pick out at random several links. Then push them towards each other and out again – there shouldn't be too much play.*

171 *Fit the chains back on to the cogs and then bolt the mechanism to the engine. After doing this fit all the tensioners and slippers/vibration dampers and replace the outer casing.*

172 *Before putting the sump on fit the oil filter holder. After the sump is in place fit and connect this pipe.*

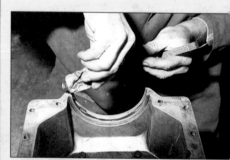

173 *Before the sump is fitted Colin put the rear seal into place. As with the top section the recess into which it fits was smeared with Blue Hylomar sealer. The cork seal was then fitted. The front seal was also put in at this stage.*

Colin fitted the timing chain cover and the sump. Note that one of the bolts that hold the front edge of the sump is shorter than the rest because one of the timing case securing bolts locates beneath it.

**NEXT MONTH
Engine rebuild continues**

PRACTICAL CLASSICS RESTORATION PROJECT
'E' type!

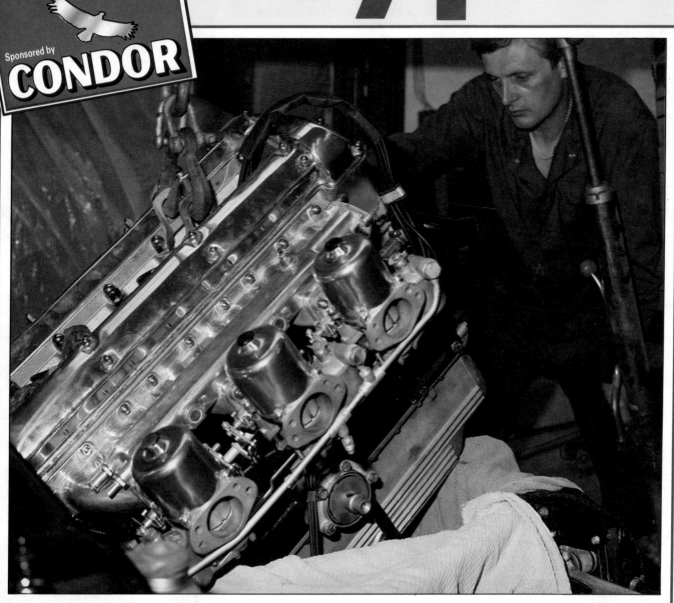

Part 15

Colin Ford assembles the top end of the engine and mates it to the block. Philip Cooper brings us the story.

PRACTICAL CLASSICS RESTORATION PROJECT

'E'type!

The work on our project 'E' type is nearing completion now and, having rebuilt the bottom end of the engine, Colin Ford (C.F. Autos, 5 South Road, Erith, Kent) now turns his attention to the head.

As I have already mentioned, this has been adapted to run on unleaded fuel with the fitment of high nickel content exhaust and inlet valve seats and bronze valve guides. The next stage is to fit the stainless steel valves.

Colin began by smearing the valve stem and lubricating the valve guide surface in each case with Graphogen assembly compound. The valves were then positioned and worked in and out to ensure their operation was smooth. It was then necessary to turn the head over to carry out the rest of the assembly. Colin used a valve support board (available from the Jaguar Enthusiasts Club – JEC) to hold the loose valves in position as the head was turned over.

After putting a valve spring seat over the valve stem Colin fitted the rubber valve seals. These are required only on the inlet side and should locate over the guide. The double valve spring was then dropped in, a valve collar was put on top and then, using a spring compressor (again available from the JEC) the spring was compressed so that the cotters could be fitted. When you're satisfied that the spring is secure, tap the end of the valve a couple of times to ensure that everything has located properly and that it's not all going to spring apart.

Next Colin removed the valve support board and fitted the shell halves for the cam, making sure that everything was very clean. Then the shims were fitted (ideally six of the smallest size) and the cam followers added after.

Before bolting in the cams we had to raise one side of the head off the table otherwise, as the cam was tightened down, the valves would lift and make contact with the table – they protrude below the level of the cylinder head when fully extended.

The cam with the drive on one end is the one to be used on the inlet side of the engine. Colin fitted this first and began by lubricating those parts of the shaft that will come into contact with the bearing shells. The bearing caps are stamped with their respective positions and must be fitted with these numbers next to the numbers on the head. The bearing shells were positioned, the cam was placed on the head and the caps were bolted down evenly and gradually. The cam was then rotated a couple of times to ensure that everything had seated correctly.

All the clearances were measured and then corrected by removing the cam and adjusting he shims underneath to suit. Never assume that any shims you buy will

174 *Colin puts the valve spring seat into place.*

176 *With the shim in place the cam follower is put on.*

178 *You should use a setting key like this (available from JEC) to get the cam in the correct position*

175 *As can be seen from this comparison, the valve springs often compress with age.*

177 *Put the timing cogs into the chains and temporarily hold them with an elastic band.*

be of the quoted size. They often vary so, to save yourself time, don't fit any unless you have checked them with a micrometer. The cam was replaced and the gap sizes double checked. It's important to note that the cam followers and shims etc. must be put back on to the same valve from which they originally came. It's possible for these, too, to have small variations in thickness and replacing them on wrong valves can lead to problems.

It's sensible to make a chart of the shims that you have fitted to both sides and also to note the valve clearances that exist. Before Colin tackled the other side he removed everything that he had just fitted explaining that, if this is not done, there would be a clash of valves. It's at this stage that a valve storage board is of great value.

The clearance on the inlet side should be 4thou compared to 6thou on the exhaust side. If you have any doubt (½thou either way) you should go for the greater gap. When both sides are done set the cam in the correct position with the engine at top dead centre, on cylinders one and six. Everything will then be correctly orientated for the distributor drive and the head can be fitted.

The block and head faces must be very clean and the gasket fitted the correct way

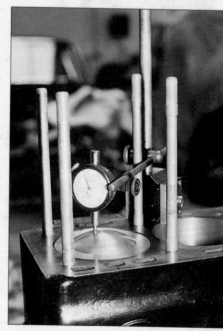
179 *We used a dial test indicator to find top dead centre accurately.*

around – it should be marked 'top'. Also make sure that all the holes in the gasket line-up with the oil channels and waterways as they should. Fit the cogs on to the timing chains and hold them together with an elastic band. Fit the water pump and engine mounts and, using the necessary spacers, fit the alternator's tensioning bracket and its mounting bracket. You can fit the jockey wheel but Colin advises that this be added later to avoid damaging the wheel during engine fitment.

The insides of the stud holes were lubricated with Copper Slip as the head is alloy

PRACTICAL CLASSICS RESTORATION PROJECT

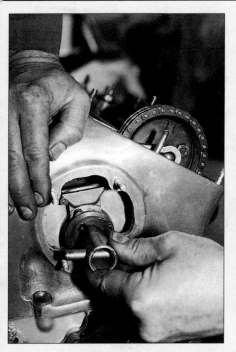

180 *Tension the chains before setting the cams. You should be able to flex the chain each side of the sprocket on both cams. Turn the sprocket anti-clockwise to tension.*

181 *After setting the cams, tighten the two bolts one at a time, turning the engine as required. Return to top dead centre and wire the bolts.*

182 *Water and deposits in the bottom of the float chamber flow through and rust this spring.*

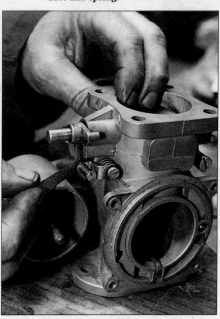

183 *With the butterfly installed and closed you should be able to fit a 2thou feeler gauge into this gap.*

184 *The shank of a ⁷⁄₁₆in drill should just contact the lever if it is set up right.*

and this will help to prevent any corrosion and seizure. The head was then fitted. Remove the elastic band from the timing cogs and, if these locate perfectly on to the cam, they can be bolted-up. If they don't, however, the circlip should be removed and the disc turned until it fits. This procedure is very well explained in the manual.

There are three types of cylinder head stud. These consist of the standard length variety and those that are slightly longer for securing the lifting brackets. Among the latter there is one that has a wider dowl at its base. This one, which is located between cylinders five and six on the exhaust side, is probably designed to ensure that the gasket sits square. The head may now be torqued-up – follow the instructions in the manual for this.

On this car Colin decided to fit the manifolds with stainless steel studs. Conventional studs rust, especially on the exhaust side, and, as much as anything else, start to look unsightly. The studs should go in easily but if they prove tight remove them and inspect. Driving them in by force may well cause them to shear. We've also used stainless

steel nuts. Fit the gaskets and the manifolds. Note that on the exhaust manifold there are three longer studs. These fit at the rear of the engine (cyl. No.1) and secure the breather pipe and dipstick holder. Finally fit the brackets and pipes from the water pump to the heater (heater return pipe), and the throttle linkage.

Next on Colin's list were the triple SU carburettors. In each case, he began by removing the dashpot damper and the dashpot that is held in place with four screws. The spring and the piston were taken out and Colin pointed out that it's best to replace the needle for the best results. However, if you choose to keep the old one, be careful not to damage it and do remove the clamping screw and reset the needle in the correct plane when you replace it.

Next he removed the return spring lever, the throttle lever at the other end, undid the two screws that hold the butterfly and withdrew the main spindle. Then the slow running valve was removed and, turning to the other side, the choke pushrod assembly was unscrewed and the pushrod withdrawn from underneath.

Having undone the four screws that secure the float chamber, the jet was withdrawn. Ideally the diaphragm should be flexible so if it has turned brittle it will need to be replaced. With the carburettor dismantled to this degree we checked that the piston lift pin was not corroded and that it moved freely. If you do strip it out, re-fit with the rubber seal, washer and circlip and check it for freedom of movement. It is not necessary to remove the jet bearing.

To re-assemble, Colin first lubricated the piston and checked that it moved freely in the dashpot. Then the piston was fitted into the housing and the large spring and screw added down the dashpot. Next the piston was lifted and allowed to fall to check for smoothness of operation and the jet was centred and tightened with a ring spanner. You may find that you have to remove and re-position the jet a number of times before you get it in the centre. Once it is centred you should hear a slight clunk as the piston is lifted and allowed to drop. The jet housing was put in place and a new spring fitted. We then tightened up the four bolts that hold this and the float chamber, ensuring that the cam was next to the push rod. The push rod should be lubricated and checked to see that it moves very freely. The bolt, spring and bracket were fitted to the other end of the pushrod.

Moving on, the next job was to grease the threads and fit the slow running valve. Screw this all the way down until it is just closed (don't tighten it at all) and then back it off two turns. The spindle bearings, sealing glands and spindle can then be fitted into the housing. The spindle bearings will need to be replaced if, when rocked from side to side within the hole, they show excessive play. You can also push them backwards and forwards to see if there is any movement on the butterfly.

Colin was then able to fit the butterfly. After making sure that it shut properly, he

PRACTICAL CLASSICS RESTORATION PROJEC

'E' type!

186   Put the clutch on. Note the drill holes in the clutch housing next to the socket where it has been balanced.

▲ 185   Once assembled this is how the triple SUs should look.

187   There are some 700 needle rollers in this gearbox which will fall out when the unit is stripped.

▼ 188   To strip the gearbox to this extent you will probably need special tools.

held it closed and tightened up the bolts – this will ensure that it remains central. A screwdriver was then used to open up the split in the screws. The final screw was then fitted into the choke pushrod assembly.

Next pull out the hinge pin in the float chamber and take out the float lever. It's well worth replacing the float needle and seating as the needle wears and becomes poorly seated which causes flooding and bad running. Colin fitted a new needle lever and pin and checked that the float lever was cutting out in the correct place before it was re-assembled with a new gasket.

After this, by screwing the mixture adjuster, Colin set the jet so that its top was level with the bridge of the carburettor. The mixture screw was then taken back 2½ turns. He then put the dashpot on to the piston and clamped it down with the four screws. Then the two gaskets and the insulator block were fitted on to the inlet manifold and the carbs were bolted into position. All the linkages and springs etc., and the fuel rail that links the carburettors together, were replaced with all the nuts and bolts being done up only finger tight. Colin was also careful to ensure that none of the springs or filters sprang out of the float chamber as the fuel rail was fitted. Fit the overflow pipes to the top of the carburettors but make sure that they don't foul any of the linkages or return springs. You can use ordinary brake pipe if you have to fabricate new overflow pipes. Bolt on the exhaust manifold.

Colin fitted the blanking plate to the rear of the block and put in a new spigot bearing. He could now offer up the flywheel. Hammer the two dowls into the block and fit the locking washer in place. Put on the remaining ten bolts.

Next wipe Graphogen or pour a little oil over the cams, apply Blue Hylomar to the gasket and fit the cam covers using copper washers. When tightening down the nuts on the cam covers, Colin used an impact socket as they have the same number of flats as the nuts and are therefore less likely to cause any damage. Alternatively you can use copper or brass insert sleeves in ordinary sockets. Colin also checked the fit of the distributor at this stage and then removed it so that he had better access to the engine mounts and to make sure it wouldn't get damaged when the engine was fitted. The clutch was next to be fitted and care was taken to ensure that it was bolted-up evenly.

As with the differential, the Jaguar gearbox is really a matter for the professional. It's sufficient to say that if you know what to do then I don't need to tell you again and if

you don't know then no amount of explanation from me is going to give you the experience you need to tackle the job.

Whichever way you approach the gearbox, the completed unit should be mated to the engine after the release fork and assembly have been well greased.

Fit the gearbox breather and complete all the necessary bracketry and pipe lines etc. Finally fit the starter motor. Once this is in place with the engine in, access to the bolts is very restricted. So, don't crank the bolts up with a ratchet before it goes in but, instead, do it up moderately tightly and then complete the tightening with a spanner once the engine has been installed. This way it won't be so tight that you can't undo it at a later date should you need to.

NEXT MONTH
Installing the engine
and fitting the trim

PRACTICAL CLASSICS RESTORATION PROJECT

'E'type!

Sponsored by
CONDOR

Part 16

It's time to install the engine and finish our 'E' type! Philip Cooper concludes the story.

PRACTICAL CLASSICS RESTORATION PROJECT
'E' type!

Having been repaired and rebuilt our 'E' type engine once again is about to grace the frames in which it belongs.

It's a monster of a unit and Colin Ford began this month by checking that the bolt threads on the engine mounts were clean and clear. He then prepared the engine for installation by removing the jockey wheel, ignition timing pointer, distributor, thermostat housing and the breather at the front of the engine.

Our list of essential tools included a good crane with as wide a spread as possible, axle stands and a trolley jack. Colin started by using the latter to get the back end of the car as high as possible. We couldn't lower the front end to increase this as the ground clearance would be insufficient. The front and rear road wheels were then removed and the car was supported on axle stands. We dismantled the front suspension and Colin used wires to hold the heavy hub in an upright position. Setting links could then be fitted – these should be used if available as a tool to ensuring that the suspension is correctly set up.

After putting the prop shaft into the transmission tunnel, Colin draped cloths over the frames and other vulnerable areas before dropping in the engine and gearbox and securing the side mounts. It looks easy on paper but in reality it is more like fitting a size 9 foot into a size 8 shoe, and that's without touching the sides! Remember also that if the cloths you use are too thick the engine just won't fit. It took us about an hour of delicate manoeuvres to get it right.

During the next stage, setting up the front suspension, we jacked up the assembly to exert a sufficient load to enable the top link and steering arm to be tightened without the ball joints revolving. We then tightened the remaining bolts, checking as we did so that their threads went through the nylon in the nyloc. Colin left the bolts that secure the top and bottom links to the frame until the car was on its wheels and correctly loaded.

With the bottom pulley on, the distributor in and set up, and all the pipes connected, we bolted the prop shaft in. We then turned our attentions to the rest of the car.

The radiator was next, along with the header tank and all the hoses etc. Colin advises that the system initially be run on ordinary water until you're sure there are no leaks. It can then be drained – this will also help flush-out any debris – and refilled with the correct mixture of water and antifreeze.

Before the mudguards were painted, rubber strips were secured around their edges. Following the necessary procedure we laid the pre-drilled metal strip on the mudguard and drilled all the holes through. The metal

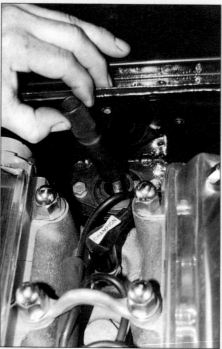

189 *This tool (Jaguar Enthusiasts Club) will help with locating the engine's rear stabiliser. Follow up by bolting in the gearbox with its spring and two rubber cups then fit the reaction plate.*

192 *Fit the carburettors and air filter. On series I cars this must be done before the aluminium splash guard is fitted.*

strip was then laid on top of the rubber and the first three holes were drilled. With this done we put the metal and rubber on to the mudguard and the first three holes were temporarily secured. We worked around the rest of the edge positioning, clamping, drilling and securing one hole at a time. We then removed the rubber, fitted the small mounting bracket and trial-fitted the mudguard. Once the fit was good the unit was removed and painted.

Body Guard 3M is a fairly flat finish anti-stone chip which we sprayed on the tyre side of the mudguard. It was then all painted black as original – some people prefer to paint them in the body colour. Once the paint had dried we replaced the rubber and bolted the mudguard in place. Until the rubber had settled Colin held it down when closing the bonnet to stop it from catching.

With regard to re-trimming, Colin says

190 *If the rubber tears when drilled use a punch. Rivets were originally used to secure this strip. We used self-tappers – easier to remove the mudguard for maintenance.*

191 *Adjust the balancing links to prevent them fouling the underside of the bonnet when shut and to avoid ground contact when open. Always ensure there's nothing under the front of the bonnet when you open it.*

that with some trim kits it's rather like buying an off-the-peg suit. They are very good value but may need a little tailoring if they are to fit perfectly. Our kit came from Barry Hankinson, Berkeley Business Centre, Brampton Street, Ross-on-Wye, Herefordshire HR9 7HF (Tel: 0989 65789).

The procedure for fitting was fairly straightforward. Colin laid the sound deadening (where applicable) and stuck it down with adhesive. In a couple of places, and in particular around the front end of the transmission tunnel, Colin had to make some light cuts in the material so that it accurately followed the contours. He also suggests that particular attention be paid to the mounting holes around which the material will have to be cut. The console which fits over the

PRACTICAL CLASSICS RESTORATION PROJECT

193 *Fit the splash guard using the bracket. Another splash guard locates in front of the radiator.*

194 *Attach the overrider extension to the front bumper, slide in a suitably cut piece of rubber and bolt up. The correct bolt must be used for this – if it's too long it may damage the chrome.*

196 *If the battery is connected when the alternator cover is fitted care must be taken to prevent a short circuit.*

197 *After the headlight fit the indicator/ sidelight unit.*

195 *Waxoyl the bonnet seams. Chrome bead tags have one flange longer than the other as do the two joining bonnet panels. Fit like to like and bend up to give a neat finish.*

transmission tunnel is fastened at the front by two brackets (one on each side) and these provide such an example. The same applies to the carpets so we punched a hole around the console bracket. However, the depth of material left the bracket a little tight so some of the surrounding backing material/sound deadening was cut away. The carpets are mostly secured with pegs that are supplied with the trim kit. The rear section of the passenger console carpet has two poppers in it!

Moving on to the front lights, Colin fitted the eight-pin connecter into place and then put all the wires into the black union/wire joint. This joint mustn't be over-tightened because it's made of bakelite which is very brittle and, more importantly, unavailable.

Vaseline was used on these connections and the eight-pin connecter as a corrosion inhibitor. The wires were then fed through the back of the headlamp bowl and, after the rubber backing had been put on, Colin fitted the unit.

A short chrome bead was fitted to the seam which bleeds from the bottom of the headlamp area. As there is no spacing washer in this seam Colin loosened the panel bolts slightly to allow the bead tags to locate through the seam. The tags were then bent over to hold the bead in place. The headlamp scoop, fitted with a rubber, was then positioned. Colin made sure that the three holes to the rear of the scoop were correctly aligned before it was all tightened up; at the front the scoop fits over the tag. The sealed

beam unit could then be slotted into place. Our headlights were the correct sealed beam Lucas units with Lucas stamped on the glass. However, not all the lamps, and even some of those in Lucas boxes, have the name stamped on the glass. Anyone going all out for originality should check for this when buying. Note also that the series I rims have key slots while the rest have holes.

Once the glue on the carpets had dried and Colin had recovered from the giddiness induced by the vapours, he tackled the door trims. The retaining clips were pushed through the door trim in their respective positions. Initially these were only half tight so that the chrome strip could be slid over them – the back edge of the clips were then fully bent over towards each other. Colin then fitted the top section of the trim to the door and clipped the main trim panel in to ensure that the clips were in the correct place. Because the securing holes (that need to be drilled) for the chrome strip are obscured by the door trim, we put the strip on and marked its position with masking tape. The strip and the trim panel were then removed and the strip was repositioned along the length of the tape, drilled and secured with self-tappers. The initial positioning of this strip is fairly critical, especially at the forward edges where the chrome has to bend slightly. Bad positioning may cause the chrome to pop out when the door is shut

PRACTICAL CLASSICS RESTORATION PROJECT
'E' type!

198 *Attach the bonnet catch and screw in the grille. Put the rubber seal around the forward edge of the bulkhead.*

199 *Use the masking tape to gauge the correct position of the chrome strip. Push the holes through for the window winder and door handle mechanisms.*

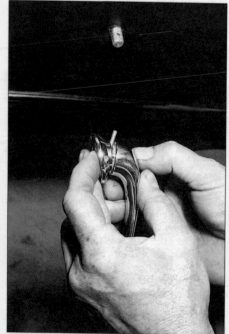

200 *Fit rubbers behind the trim to the window winder and door handle to keep them padded out.*

201 *Re-covering the centre console is straightforward but tedious and fiddly. It was necessary to put a hole in the correct position for the seat belt mounts.*

To fit the seats Colin punched holes in the floorpan Hardura so that the two fixing bosses could be screwed in to the captive nuts in the floorpan. The runners fit over these bosses and are screwed to the floor at the rear. It's worth noting that some reproduction floorpans have four holes at the front for the bosses to cater for both the 3.8 and the 4.2 models – make sure that you punch the holes through the Hardura in the correct place!

To complete the interior, and indeed the car, the arm rests were put on to the doors after the captive nuts had been thoroughly greased. If these seize it won't be possible to remove the arm rest which, in turn, would prevent the door trim from being taken off. Colin also notes that if the arm rest isn't tightened sufficiently, over time and with use, the screws will bend. However, care must be taken to prevent overtightening which will crack the plastic.

202 *Fitting the carpets. Note the hole around the centre console bracket.*

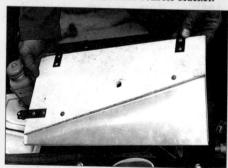

203 *Don't forget the two heat deflectors that fit underneath the car.*

Next Month
Assessing the car and counting the costs.

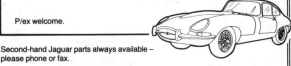

Discover JAGUAR

QUARTERLY

If you've never seen a copy of *Jaguar Quarterly* you simply don't know what you're missing. Edited by Paul Skilleter, it's a full-colour, 134-page magazine devoted entirely to Jaguar, covering the full spectrum of models from SS to XJ and including:

● Historic features ● New-car tests and descriptions ● Classic Jaguar values ●
Technical features ● Track tests, modified Jaguar reports ● Worldwide Jaguar news
including racing ● Factory visits and interviews ● Trade and specialist news ●
Fascinating dealer & private ads

Since *Jaguar Quarterly* was established in 1988 it has received worldwide recognition. *Jaguar Quarterly* is entirely independent of Jaguar Cars Ltd but enjoys the full confidence of the Company and works closely with it.

SUBSCRIBE NOW! One-year (four-issue) subscription rates are £14.50 UK/BFPO, or overseas via air-lifted delivery: £17 Europe, USA $29, Canada $33, Australia $A45, NZ $50; all other countries £21. Rates valid to end 1991. Please enquire after this date OR send £2.95 for post-free sample issue (UK only).

SPECIAL 'E' TYPE SOUVENIR ISSUE! Published April 1991, this contains unique material on the 'E' type, including contemporary colour photographs and drawings never published before, easy-reference facts and figures, restoration and buying information. A unique momento of the 'E' type's 30th year that is bound to become a collector's item. Included as part of a four-issue subscription or available singly at £2.95 post-free (UK only), or £5.00 inclusive of postage overseas (credit card or sterling cheque drawn on British bank only for single issue).

JUST FILL IN THE FORM BELOW and send to **PJ Publishing Ltd., PO Box 40, Hornchurch, Essex RM11 3LG. (Tel/Fax: 04024 75993).**

- -

I would like to subscribe to *Jaguar Quarterly* commencing with the current issue OR I require a single current copy at £2.95 (UK only).
FAX no: 04024 75993.

Please find my cheque enclosed for £ ....
OR:-
Please charge my VISA/MASTERCARD No: _____

Expires _____   Signature _____

Name: _____   Address: _____

_____

Fax acceptable if paying by credit card. Photocopy/letter acceptable.

E/1ED

PRACTICAL CLASSICS RESTORATION PROJECT

'E' type!

Sponsored by **CONDOR**

Part 17

It was in early 1989 that our 'E' type restoration project was born but it is only now, after much demanding work, that Philip Cooper can provide the final report!

PRACTICAL CLASSICS RESTORATION PROJECT

'E' type!

The 'E' type Jaguar has on numerous occasions been praised for its elegant lines, performance, style and much besides. However, few journals have ever touched upon maintenance or repair in any detail and one wonders why. It is, after all, regarded by many as the greatest sportscar of all time and it's British at that! How fitting then that it is this magazine which has put the record straight and tackled every aspect of the car in a full restoration.

At the start our first choice would have been a roadster. However, as luck would have it, an increasingly buoyant market was boosted by investment prospectors and prices soared beyond our means. Asking prices in the region of £15,000 for very rough, genuine RHD convertibles for restoration were not uncommon (this figure has almost halved now). Consequently we changed tack, settled on the fixed head

204 *The abundance of chromework, both inside and out, really highlights the car's traditional feel and appearance.*

205 *Comprehensive instrumentation, leather bound interior as original.*

206 *The engine is quiet, extremely smooth and looks great.*

coupe (series one, of course) and purchased LAY 394E for a rather more palatable £7,500.

It was then down to Colin Ford of CF Autos in Kent to resuscitate the tired old vehicle and breath fresh spirit back into its delapidated being. What a task that proved to be!

Those who saw the car at the 1989 Bromley Pageant of Motoring will know what a sorry state it was in before work began. Nevertheless, Colin was undaunted and tackled the challenge with vigour. Early on it became apparent that the car had suffered accident damage. Both the nearside and the roof were battered and one of the first decisions made was to replace, rather than repair, the roof panel. In the event this was very successful. A new bonnet was also fitted in place of the rusty and damaged original. A number of smaller panels, plus the rear chassis legs, were also replaced and the car was treated to two new doors, a complete boot floor section and repair arches for the inner and outer rear wings. It was also more economic to replace the thoroughly rusted outer and inner sills on both sides of the car and, in fact, the complete floor and part of the rear bulkhead were also replaced.

With bodywork repairs complete Colin painted the car. Eight litres of two-pack Jaguar British Racing Green, supplied by Glasurit Paints of West Drayton, were sprayed on after the self etch primer and the high build primer had been applied. Colin could

207 *Period pumps for a period car.*

PRACTICAL CLASSICS RESTORATION PROJECT

'E'type!

then move on to the next problem – the engine.

The original block was very badly cracked and also showed signs of previous repairs. Could we remedy the damage and re-use the original block? Luckily, the answer was yes if we used an established method of repair, first developed in the dockyards. The effect of this was to 'stitch up' and seal the crack and the other previously repaired damage. The block was then pressure-tested and to date, some 2000 miles on, has shown no sign of leakage.

The price of parts for this project exceeded £16,000, of which about a quarter was spent on panels alone. A list of approximate prices of the larger panel items includes the bonnet costing £1500, doors at £300 each, the rear boot assembly at £250 and two sets of inner and outer sills at £150. Other large items, approximately priced, include the engine repair at £450, engine machining at £2000, trim at £1400, plating and polishing at £2000. Paint and materials cost £600, a set of wheels £700, rear axle rebuild £1000, gearbox rebuild £275, not forgetting the radiator rebuild at £200 and the exhaust system at £350 which came from Bells Silencer Services Ltd of Swindon. (Tel: 0793 520866).

However, it was our experience, and it will be the experience of those who follow, that a number of parts for the car proved extremely elusive. Tracking these down caused the most delay of all.

Thankfully many companies still cater for the older car. One example is Vintage Tyre Supplies Ltd, 12 Dalston Gardens, Honeypot Lane, Stanmore, Middlesex HA7 1BY (Tel: 081-206 0722), who supply tyres from as early as 1898 and whose tyres were used on our car. We chose Dunlop Sport 185 VR 15s to match those originally fitted to the car when it left the factory in 1967.

Over the 12-month restoration period the car was transformed from a rusted and tatty wreck to a fantastic 'E' type Jaguar of the finest quality. I quote a reader's description of Colin Ford's work: "To me he has forged the link between art and science with what he has done to the car." What more need I say?

208 *The paintwork is excellent but the beauty of the Jaguar is much more than skin deep.*

Specifications

Cubic capacity	4235cc
Max. power	265bhp
Carburettors	3½in SU HD8
Weight	25.1cwt
0-60mph	7.0 secs
Top speed	150mph
Average mpg	18.5

Living with a legend

Whether you love or hate the Jaguar 'E' type there is no denying that it is a true thoroughbred among cars. It's perhaps the most famous sports car in the world and one that never fails to be recognised and admired.

Recently I was fortunate enough to 'borrow' our 1967 Series 1 4.2 fhc model and, frankly, I'm still glowing from the experience! The car was quite simply a joy to live with and drive. Even just to stand looking at it gave me immense pleasure – its sleek lines and sheer presence leave you in no doubt as to its purpose.

Climbing in over the wide sill you settle into a compact interior and are faced with an impressive array of white on black instrumentation. The comfortable but firm seats are, of course, trimmed in leather and the whole 'feel' is very traditional. The steering wheel is wood-rimmed, large and spindly, the gear lever, to the left, stands high and proud and the handbrake is mounted, apparently awkwardly, still further away on the far side of the carpeted tunnel. The view forward is dominated by the bulging bonnet and is rather daunting at first. It's impossible to see the front (or the back come to that) from the driver's seat but push the starter button to fire the engine and all such grievances are soon forgotten.

Around town the car is totally manageable so long as adequate allowance is made for that expensive nose! Seek out some country roads, though, and the 'E' type comes alive. The beautifully smooth straight-six motor punches out seemingly endless reserves of power. Acceleration is impressive and still sufficient to deal with most on the road, apart from those with 'supercar' performance.

I did not find the steering as precise as I had hoped but the overall ride is very good. On fast bends the car is prone to understeer initially but, assuming you have chosen the right line and you hold on to it (together with your nerve!), more power can be applied to balance the car on the throttle, after which it will settle and leave the corner at a great rate of knots! It is the type of car which has to be driven 'enthusiastically' for the best results. Easing off halfway through a corner is not the 'E' type way. Fling it about a bit and it'll really work for you! It's utterly predictable and very safe when treated with respect.

This is certainly a car that I would love to own and one that I would feel happy about driving on any occasion – it really is a credit to Colin Ford's expertise and tremendous attention to detail. There are dated aspects, of course, as you would expect – the lights are weak, the heater grumbles and the wipers are barely adequate in heavy rain – but these niggles are all forgivable. It's a pure driving machine with bags of character, style and outright brute force. What more could any enthusiast wish for? Even today, in the age of the computer-designed car, the E's timelessly beautiful lines are still a magnet to passers by, whether they are old or young. Everyone *just knows* it's an 'E' type. A quite superb car! *CAG*

The Jaguar Enthusiasts' Club offer so much to all Jaguar enthusiasts:

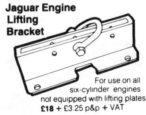

Prices correct as at January 1991

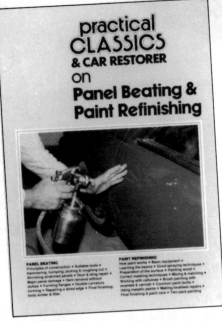